GOING DEAF FOR A LIVING

GOING DEAF FOR A LIVING

STEVE LAMACQ

OMNIBUS PRESS

London / New York / Paris / Sydney / Copenhagen / Berlin / Madrid / Tokyo

Cover designed by Raissa Pardini.
Picture research by the author.

ISBN: 9781787601277
Order No: OP57849

Exclusive Distributors
Music Sales Limited
14/15 Berners Street
London W1T 3LJ

'A Song From Under The Floorboards'
Lyrics by Howard Devoto.
© Copyright Mute Song Ltd.
Used by permission.

Designed and typeset by Evolution Design and Digital Ltd (Kent)
Printed in the Czech Republic.

A catalogue record for this book is available from the British
Library.

Visit Omnibus Press at **www.omnibuspress.com**

Contents

Intro

The Old Red Lion in Kennington, South London, where the bulk of this book was originally written, was bought out a few years ago and renovated.

I'd say they 'tarted it up', but actually 'retro-ed it out' might be a better description. They went for that auction house, distressed furniture look, which has been a popular trend across London over the past decade. All exposed brickwork and board games.

I can tell you this for certain as I'm writing this while I'm sat at a table where the gents toilet used to be (because my old corner, the one where I used to fritter away Sunday lunchtimes, is now a kitchen). And it's only just really struck me that although I occasionally get nostalgic for the Old Man's pub which it used to be, with its ageing clientele – who moved on pretty quickly, post refurb – I actually feel pretty comfortable here now.

There have been a lot of changes but it's still very familiar, which in many ways is how I feel about the music business, and my own little corner of it.

Going Deaf For A Living was originally published in the autumn of 2000, to mark the tenth anniversary of the Radio 1 show *The Evening Session*, in an age when there were still two weekly music papers and *Top Of The Pops* on the telly.

We bought music mostly on CD, the 12-inch single having become the preserve of the club scene, and we were still coming to terms with the impact of mass emails and the concept of downloading. It feels like another world (in the same way that the Old Red Lion's habit of handing around free roasties to its regulars back in the nineties now feels like something quaint, but weirdly dated – like the scene in a slightly bent Polaroid picture that you've found lodged down the back of a shelf).

But while the way we buy, or 'consume', music has changed (dramatically in some cases), our relationship with it is quite often the same. I can't speak for the generations after me, some of whom won't have had the pivotal moments of their life soundtracked by a band or a scene. But, looking at the world from 6 Music, where I currently reside, it seems that a lot of us want the same things from music that we always did. All that's changed is how we access it, or, in the live context, experience it.

So (I hope) the premise of this book still holds true, even though some of the scenarios have massively altered or evolved. It is not a history of music by any means. It has some history in it, but it's a history of my pop world and the media enclave I eventually ended up in. But even then, it's my own skewed vision of it.

And it's not really about the artists mentioned either, but more my attempt to explain the relationship we have with them and how I've felt about their lives and music while watching them from a distance; while trying to make some sense of it all, which I think is something we've all probably done at one point or another.

When we were discussing the book the first time round, there was talk of calling it 'The Story Of A Music Fan', because that's really what it is. Even though, as a fan, I've been lucky enough to make something of a career out of writing about or playing records, I'm still – as you'll read – an awkward participant in the business. I'm definitely someone who has blagged themselves backstage and is still waiting for security to lead them away.

But till that happens I've carried on doing various radio shows, and I'd been trying to stay out of trouble until the opportunity came along to republish this book, off the back of a one-man show I've started touring, featuring some of the fantastical theories and familiar anecdotes you'll find in the forthcoming pages.

And it's been strange revisiting this book, as I imagine it's strange for bands who are faced with doing anniversary reissues of old albums, which they originally released when they still had hair and stayed up till 4 a.m. every night on tour. In fact, that's probably what this is. The debut album, remastered, with a bonus track – or in this case a bonus chapter.

I went back and made a few factual adjustments to it. But otherwise, in the spirit of a reissue – and despite the temptation to repaint the 'old' me in a better light – it's just as it was: a snapshot of the time; a roll call of the music that made me and the music that played a huge part in shaping the nineties.

It ends just before my old Radio 1 show, *The Evening Session*, was given the axe. And so it is, I guess, Episode One of a two-part story (with Part Two to follow, if more than five of you part with hard cash to wade through this).

In fact, it is, a bit like the Old Red Lion, less tarted up, but more retro-ed out. It certainly has a lot of distressed furniture in it.

CHAPTER 1

Ain't Got A Clue

It's just gone five o'clock and there are two of us, standing outside the backstage door at the Ipswich Gaumont. The one with glasses and a parka is me, the other one with glasses and carrying a variety of record sleeves is Graham Diss, who I sit next to in double history at school.

Inside the building, and we know they're there because we can hear them soundchecking, are The Undertones. The real, in the flesh, live Undertones. The same Undertones whose logo appears on our history roughbooks and who we've seen on *Top Of The Pops* doing 'My Perfect Cousin'. Graham Diss even has one of their hits, 'Jimmy Jimmy', on green vinyl, which makes me obscenely jealous.

Some minutes later the noise of soundchecking stops and the stage door opens to reveal two fellas looking a little flustered. HELP! One of them is Feargal Sharkey, the band's singer; the other we deduce is the tour manager. Just as we're about to pounce on them they disappear back inside and we return disconsolately to our game of kicking stones round the car park.

Another five minutes pass and the TM is back. "Do either of you two know where Radio Orwell is?"

"Yeah, I do. It's about five minutes' walk." I've got one up on Graham Diss at this point because I spend every other Saturday hanging around record shops in Ipswich.

"Can you tell us where it is, only we're supposed to be doing an interview there," the TM adds, only in retrospect it sounds more like: "Well bloody give us the directions, will you, because we're late."

"Well, if you want," I say, trying to sound cool, but stuttering slightly, "I'll take you up there."

And that is how I came to save The Undertones tour.

Of the many features we ran on *The Evening Session* on Radio 1 in the nineties, the most successful was 'Do You Remember The First Time?' It was a simple enough idea (and not a new one) but it ran for ages. All you had to do was write in and tell us about the night you lost your gig virginity. Which band did you see? Did the earth move? The mailbag was absolutely stuffed for weeks.

There were tales of lost tickets and broken limbs, the vagaries of public transport, there were family disputes (usually with elder brothers or sisters), and then explosive accounts of the headlining band walking on and playing an immaculate set which included every song the listener had wanted to hear… and more.

The question is, were any of these accounts actually true? They were true in the minds of the letter writers, but you exaggerate your first gig, don't you? If not at the time, then at least in later years. Or maybe exaggerate is the wrong word. What I've found is that we personalise them, and make them revolve more around ourselves. This is why everyone's first gig story will have different highlights – even if they happen to have broken their duck on the same night watching the same band.

Your first gig is also a subject that's guaranteed to crop up when you're sizing up new friends or acquaintances, like your first single or the first band you pinned a picture of on your wall. It's a good barometer of age, taste and attitude. It's like fingerprinting for pop fans. Although it is one of the most common experiences we have, everyone's tale is unique.

But there are parts of the story that we will allow ourselves to share, parts of the excitement and the trauma. Which is why I have honed my first gig story into a shape I'm happy with. It was a band called The Lurkers – a second-wave punk group whose third single, 'Ain't Got A Clue', had unbelievably been made Record Of The Week on Kid Jensen's Radio 1 drivetime programme. They were without question my favourite band of the era (I'd been too young for the first wave of punk and was scrabbling around for the best of the rest when I found The Lurkers on the radio). I didn't have their album yet, but I did have permission from mum and dad to go and see them at the Chancellor Hall in Chelmsford, a venue better known for its amateur dramatics and wrestling nights.

Now, blow by blow, minute by minute, I couldn't tell you exactly what happened when the gig finally arrived. But this is how I tell the story. Stop me if you recognise any similarities with your own first gig experiences:

I spent two hours before leaving deciding what to wear.

Mum and dad gave me a lift and dropped me off – not outside the venue, because that would have been too embarrassing – but at the end of the street.

They both raised their eyebrows as they surveyed the motley collection of Essex punks, students and oddballs who made up the queue outside. At least I think they raised their eyebrows. I don't think I actually saw them do it – after all, I was in the backseat of the car, and unless I was scouring the driver's mirror for a reaction, I wouldn't have been able to see them. But they definitely shifted in their seats a little, which is a sure sign of eyebrow reaction.

I had a ticket and no one else seemed to. I was quite chuffed when it had turned up in the post. Ticket number 0012. I thought this made me one of the elite (surely the lower the ticket number, the cooler you are?). Little did I realise that advance ticket sales for The Lurkers were probably in the region of 30. And that when a bouncer shouted "Anyone with tickets can come straight through," I would be the only person to shuffle from the queue and walk in, past the scornful looks of the rabble in front of me.

At the end of the night, there was a piercing ringing sound in my ears. I actually thought they were broken; that I'd done some irreparable damage to them. I was so scared that my parents might ban me from further gigs if they found out that I kept schtum. It took two and a half days for the noise to stop.

The actual details of the gig aren't that important. But being older and wiser now, I wince at the vision of the unhip me, who got to the gig too early; stood right at the front; got spat on by the singer of the support band – a local Essex group called The Sods; and was then crushed against the front of the stage as The Lurkers arrived and everyone tumbled onto the floor from the bar.

I scrambled out halfway through the set and watched the rest of the gig from beside the PA, but it was too late to save myself. I was infected with something more virulent than whatever might have been lurking in the singer's saliva. I had contracted some kind of live music disease. I know it sounds ridiculous, but I honestly think that The Lurkers at the Chancellor Hall was the most exciting moment of my life up to that point. I mean, there wasn't much to compare it to (winning a school art competition and getting a Christmas card from Linda Audsley were good, but they weren't a patch on The Lurkers). And from the moment I left the gig, all I wanted to do was go to another one. And another one.

And that's where my problems began. Living in a small Essex village, ten miles from Colchester, didn't give you much opportunity to join the live circuit. No one seemed to play in Colchester or Chelmsford – or even further up the A12 in Ipswich. On reflection, there must have been gigs going on, but either I didn't know about them or there were reasons (school, lack of transport, poor finances) that must have prevented me from going. The worst disappointment of all was that The Undertones were due to play the Chancellor Hall a month after The Lurkers… and having kept quiet about the business with the faulty ears, my parents had once again agreed to give me a lift there. Then with just days to go before Gig Two, the show was cancelled. I cursed and sulked and sat back on my bed and waited impatiently to see when they would tour next.

In the end it was three years before The Undertones finally played near enough for me to see them on a non-school night. And by that point, the entire musical landscape had changed.

Punk had been and gone, and what remained of the new wave was an overexcitable and underachieving mess. The onset of the eighties signalled a tawdry Top 40, which, apart from the odd 2 tone or Jam single, was full of charlatans and chancers as far as I could see. A bunch of FAKES. And being a teenager whose only take on pop music came through the radio and the pages of a paper called *Record Mirror*, I didn't understand what was going on. Who was responsible for this? Why had all the bands I liked started to go out of fashion? What was I going to do now?

But the worst moment of all – the point when I knew that punk and new wave were really, finally, all over – was when the Big Boys stopped going to the youth club. Every Essex village has two Big Boys. They're compulsory. They're there as a reference point for your parents and so they can say things like "You don't want to end up like them."

But at 13 you do want to end up like them, and I wanted to end up like one of them in particular because he had a leather jacket and an amazing record collection. Each week the Big Boys would idly slouch into the youth club, flick a couple of small children to the floor, and then march up and commandeer the record player.

Before discovering John Peel, they were responsible for much of my musical education (even if it was just Sham 69 and The Smirks and 999). Also, to break up the monotony of village life, the youth club would hold discos every month or so, and the Big Boys would pogo and I'd stand in the corner and gawp at them. Then one week they stopped going. And the next week it was wall-to-wall Bee Gees records and that was that. The mighty punk revolution, which had promised so much, had fallen at the first hurdle. It had lost the battle for the Colne Engaine youth club record player.

And I think I could have handled this, if I hadn't invested so heavily in music in the previous couple of years. But after The Lurkers gig I'd started to use pop music as a cover for my lack of real identity. I wasn't particularly gregarious, I wasn't terrifically good at sport, and I wasn't even that good at being the sort of swot who never seems to try but gets great marks. I was the classic OK pupil in the top stream of an OK Essex comprehensive who one day wanted to be something, but didn't know what it was he wanted to be.

The nearest I got to being enigmatic was when our frightening English teacher set our group an end of term crossword competition.

"And 14 down," she hollered, "is for you Lamacq." The clue was 'Murderous group (10 letters)'. It wasn't much of a deification, but it was enough to give me a certain amount of notoriety for a time.

But something was definitely missing. And if I had to pinpoint it, I think it was the lack of interaction between me and pop music. I bought records and taped songs off the radio and stuck pictures on my wall, but that's just being an armchair supporter (or, in reality, a lying-on-the-bed sort of supporter). No, we needed to work on this relationship between pop and me because it was too one-way.

Then sometime in 1981 The Undertones came to Ipswich on their 'Positive Touch' tour and I met Feargal Sharkey. During the walk to Radio Orwell I was barely able to speak for fear of saying something stupid. This is a situation that I can happily report has never changed to this day.

I can talk to musicians when there's a microphone around, but say I saw one of them walking through an airport – and trust me this *has* happened – I would probably duck behind an escalator to avoid them. The problem with these chance meetings with pop stars is that you know you've only got a limited amount of time with them (in Feargal's case a five-minute walk). So where do you start? People have chat-up lines for the opposite sex, but 70 years after inventing rock'n'roll, no one's come up with an infallible chat-up line for singers in bands. One that will leave them with a good impression of you.

My friend Chris The Pilot tells the story of seeing his idol Paul Weller walking towards him down Great Titchfield Street one day. Chris, as you would, is desperate to explain to Weller how important his music has been to him. But how do you shrink years of being a fan into one sentence (one that sounds genuine and well-informed). And as he's trying to concoct the words he wants to say, Weller is getting ever closer.

Then in a moment of blind panic, his mind having gone blank, just as they are about to pass, The Pilot steps in front of The Modfather… and *salutes him*.

Weller looks him up and down and says: "You alright mate?"

So what was I going to say. More than that, what did I *want* to say to Feargal anyway? Still haven't forgiven you for cancelling

Chelmsford? Any new songs in the set tonight? By the way, what are the publishing deductions like in your EMI contract?

No, I think all I wanted to say was thanks for making good records. Thanks for still being there when so many of my other favourite groups had already given up the ghost. "Cheers, Feargal, you've saved my life." Or maybe not. I think I managed a strangled enquiry about how the tour was going and then fell silent again. Within minutes Feargal was inside Radio Orwell, and Graham and I were on the pavement outside looking in.

But despite the lack of any real exchange, we were jubilant. Come the gig, we could stand in Row F and look up and say, "That's our mate Feargal. We were chatting to him this afternoon."

My lust for interaction had been cured.

As a postscript to this, when we invited listeners to send in stories about meeting their favourite or most influential pop heroes, I received an email from an Oasis fan who lived near Aberdeen. The teenager in question had been on his way back to school after his lunchtime break when he ran across the road and was nearly mown down by an impressive – not to say incongruous – limo.

As he gathered himself up from the road where he'd fallen, he saw the passenger window wind down and a head poke out. It was a concerned Noel Gallagher. "Watch yourself, man," Noel said, "you could get killed doing that."

Now, honestly, what wouldn't you give to be nearly run over by your guitar hero?

CHAPTER 2

Bubblegum

Have you ever wanted a haircut like someone in a band? And if you have, did you end up going to the hairdresser with a picture of the pop star in question and saying: "I WANT TO LOOK LIKE THIS"?

Then I hate to tell you, but you're in trouble. You're on the slippery slope. Your relationship with pop music and fashion has gone past the point of no return. You are showing signs of becoming infatuated. Your life is suddenly not your own any more.

And I should know because I've been there. At 13 I decided I wanted a haircut like the bass player from The Skids (the bass player!!!). I took the sleeve of their 'Into The Valley' single to the hairdresser in town and pointed at it. He looked at my head and gave out a curious sound that I later discovered was exactly like an electrician giving an estimate on rewiring your house. Fair play, he made a go of it, and I'm sure he wasn't lacking in barbershop skills, but when he'd finished and I looked in the mirror, I still wasn't the bass player from The Skids.

I gave up on trying to look like people in bands after that. But other aspects of my appearance – my whole outlook on life, to be honest – were changing. When I was ten I wanted to be a DJ (and you can blame the Radio 1 Roadshows and me being a reclusive only child during the summer holidays for that). Then I wanted to draw Marvel comics. Then, as I tripped over the tail end of punk, my only ambition was to live in London. Hopefully near a Tube station.

There is an interesting passage in *A Beat Concerto*, The Jam's official biography by Paolo Hewitt, describing Paul Weller's early life in Woking. Interesting to me anyway, because although Colne Engaine wasn't suburbia and I didn't want to be a guitarist, there were definite similarities between Weller and the Boy Lamacq in their early teens. Hewitt describes how Weller would make trips up to town with an old-school radio cassette recorder, and when people asked him what he was doing, Weller used to say, "I'm going to *record* London."

And it wasn't just this obsession with London – where, in our young repressed minds, everything was happening – that connected us. Hewitt also reveals how Weller's circle of friends began to change, the more obsessed he became with music and then his band. Back in Essex, the same thing was happening to me. As I wandered through my teens, I found I knew more about The Vapors than I did about who was top of the Football League. I stopped going to watch matches with my dad and used to spend the long Saturday afternoons in record shops instead.

It was obvious that as my own interests began to move on, then my circle of friends would too. It set a pattern for the rest of my life, if I'm honest about it. But that's the deal with being a pop fan. You start to choose your friends through music – or, in some cases, music chooses them for you.

And this is what happened with Maggot. Maggot was a couple of years older than me, and, I later found out, worked in the old DHSS office in Colchester. His nickname had attached itself to him at school – when his hobby was fishing – but he'd kept it anyway, probably because it sounded quite punk.

We first met at the 100 Club one night, after striking up a conversation because we were both standing on our own and were bored between bands. It transpired that we lived quite close to each other in villages on opposite sides of Colchester and shared a similar taste in music (we liked The Newtown Neurotics, The Clash and Action Pact). But there was other good bonding material between us. Maggot had already done a hundred glamorous things that a gig novice like myself had only dreamed of: he'd missed the last train back to Colchester and slept in the toilets at Liverpool Street station; he'd met one of Peter & The Test Tube Babies.

Maggot's favourite story was of a punk gig in Norwich where, to quell the threat of violence, the promoters had forced everyone entering the venue to take the laces out of their boots. The only problem was that they threw all the laces in a cardboard box, which meant no one knew which were whose. At the end of the night they put the box at the exit... and there was a full-scale fight over a rather nice set of red DM ones.

This was the downside to gigs in the early to mid-eighties that sometimes gets forgotten: the smell of trouble that hung in the air at many punk gigs. We were used to occasional grief in Colchester – mostly at the hands of squaddies from the local barracks – but in London the second-wave punk shows could be dark and scary affairs. Travelling in twos helped allay fears that you would leave for home with the imprint of a skinhead's fist down the side of your cheek.

So Maggot and I became Essex County's most well-travelled gig-goers. I had old school and college friends – some good mates – but Maggot was my link with the world outside education and family. He started writing for my fanzine – *A Pack Of Lies*, which was my first venture into print – and we even went out and followed bands round on tour (sleeping in my car to save money – I always lost the toss and got the front seat with the handbrake biting into my ribs). One night, parked in a lay-by near Sunderland, we were woken by two bullish Military Police officers who thought we were two squaddies on the run. One flash of the torch at the creature lying under a donkey jacket across the back seat was enough to convince them that we weren't. That was Maggot. We lost touch when I started work and the music scene began to evolve, but I'm sure if we met now, we'd talk about the same nonsense.

And that's the point. You can meet people by chance who you were at school with for years and shared some of your most traumatic times with and not have more than three questions to ask them. The conversation is stilted and uncomfortable and set in the past. But meet somebody who you know through music, and there's always some common ground.

I keep in touch with a couple of my college friends – noticeably the ones who were most into records – but the mid-eighties for me are marked out by people I met while I was writing or selling my fanzine. I can – and have – gone for years without seeing them, but sooner or later they pop up again and you just carry on where you left off (can you imagine that happening with old next-door neighbours or workmates?).

A good example of this is Laurence Bell. When I started *A Pack Of Lies* I filched many of my ideas from an Ipswich-based fanzine called *Harsh Reality*, which had folded just before my first issue came back from the printers. Then one afternoon in Parrot Records I was trying to persuade the assistant behind the counter to stock my latest issue when a young chap picked up a copy and began flicking through it.

"What's this then?" he asked with a nice mix of enthusiasm and nonchalance.

"It's my fanzine. It's like a Colchester version of *Harsh Reality*. Look, see that bit, I nicked that from *Harsh Reality*…"

Smiling, he nodded his head. I felt the full sales pitch building up, so I forged on: "Do you remember *Harsh Reality* at all?"

"Remember it?" he grinned. "I wrote it."

"YOU'RE LAURENCE!"

And that was it. We chatted for a while, I offloaded ten copies of issue four on the shop's assistant manager and I didn't see Laurence again for years. Then one night I went to see a band called The Adicts at the 100 Club in London. And, to my amazement, who should be the singer in the support band Perfect Daze? It was Laurence. This time we kept in touch for a while and when I joined *NME* (*New Musical Express*) I wrote a couple of favourable reviews of the Daze, who went on to gig with several fashionable Ipswich skate-punk bands and released a handful of energetic pop-punk singles.

Then, inevitably, we lost touch again. I don't know why. A couple of unreturned calls, then you lose a phone number and then your life fills up with other people. And then I was out with Dave Bedford from Fire Records one night who told me about their plans to start a new guitar offshoot label. It was going to be run by some chap they'd found who knew all there was to know about the American scene and had a good ear for a tune. "Can't tell you who it is at the moment – it's a secret," added Bedford conspiratorially, "but he really knows his stuff."

"His name's not Laurence, is it?"

"How did you know that?!"

"Just a guess." And so Laurence started the great Roughneck Records and lived in London and he used to drop round to the *NME* with his latest releases by Leatherface or The Lemonheads and it was nice to have him around again – and have someone to stand with at gigs. I think there were another six months when the phone calls dried up (later explained by his departure from Fire to start his own label, Domino Records, which over the past 25 years has flourished into one of the UK's best known and most respected independent labels, finding mainstream success with bands like Franz Ferdinand and Arctic Monkeys, but now equally known for its experimental electronic music and adventures in alt-folk). But apart from that gap, we've done pretty well and we'll still end up going to gigs, Laurence as hungry for and inquisitive about new music as he's ever been.

Laurence – and a few others – make up some sort of loose gang of old friends who are also fans: people who hopefully forgive me being useless at returning calls and understand that our shared lunacy when it comes to music is enough to cement our friendship. I haven't checked, but at least two of them definitely did that thing with the picture and the hairdresser.

Back at Halstead's Ramsey School, it wasn't hard picking mates into music. You just had to know where to sit in class.

The Ramsey School obeyed the universal laws of seating arrangements based on musical taste: i.e. boy band-supporting pop kids at the front, the obscurest indie fans and metalheads at the back. You can't place the dance fans, because they keep moving about. And I know some schools flout these laws, but it's not a bad rule of thumb. We all had to sit somewhere near the back because the logos of the bands we liked were more complicated to draw than everyone else's. Some of them could take an entire geography lesson to do. Then there's the business with making lists (Top 10 current favourite singles, Top 10 all-time best bands, and the Top 10 records I would like to buy if I could get a decent Saturday job to pay for them). It's no wonder I didn't get round to filling in those entry forms for university. I was too busy working out which was the all-time greatest Blondie single.

The fact that I'd decided not to go to uni, though, made me something of a pariah in the eyes of my school. Out of all the pupils in the upper sixth, I was the only one who didn't get the traditional end-of-school interview with the headmaster. Mind you, it could also have been because a month before the end of term I strode out to bat in the sixth form versus teachers cricket match, dressed not in the regulation whites but in black DMs, black jeans and a T-shirt which bore the legend 'Chronic Generation'. I hit a four off my English tutor and was out for six.

Instead of university, I'd passed the entrance exam for a course in journalism run from Harlow College. And, of course, within a week of arriving, I'd handpicked most of my best friends to be based on either: a) geographical location – a couple of them came from around Colchester; or b) musical taste. It's important to add that in some cases it doesn't matter WHICH bands people like, as long as they like them with the same, insane, obsessive approach that I have. My new best mate was Greg Fountain, son of an important PR man at Vauxhall Motors in Luton, who lived and breathed Bob Dylan. I knew I had made a good choice in Greg when, within a couple of months of the course starting, we had to bunk off college one day and drive to Luton to buy the new Dylan LP *Infidels* on the day of release. A day later wouldn't have been any good.

And I couldn't abide Bob Dylan. But then again Greg wasn't a big fan of Welsh punk band The Partisans either, so the arrangement worked quite well. The most important aspect of living in Harlow, however, was that I was finally in striking distance of gigs in London. Once, maybe twice a week, I'd walk a mile through the town park to the train station and head for the Smoke. Financially this would have been a struggle, but I soon discovered that there was never a ticket inspector at Harlow station to greet the last train home. So all you needed was a single to town and you were sorted.

It was a rule that failed only once. One night, ticketless and penniless, I began walking towards to the exit before spotting the orange bib of an inspector who obviously didn't have a home to go to. Panicking slightly, I was forced to turn back to the platform and make good my escape (this involved leaping over two sets of live rails, scaling the wall into the Post Office car park and then sprinting to safety).

I wasn't the only one who occasionally diddled the ticket inspectors. On my third Harlow–London expedition I met ranting poet and writer Attila The Stockbroker at Liverpool Street station. I introduced myself as a local fanzine writer and asked if he'd like a hand carrying his bags and mandolin. "No thanks, I'll be needing these," he said, as he set off like an overburdened mum with too much shopping. The guards simply looked at him sympathetically as he made a failed attempt to find a ticket, and waved him on his way.

We chatted on the train home, and I got his phone number. And through him I found The Newtown Neurotics, the only band I'd heard of from Harlow. I didn't realise quite the impact that meeting them would have on me, but then I hadn't taken stock of where my interest in music was really going. The Neurotics unlocked a new underground world for me – at the same time as the rest of the UK student population was busy 'saving' the overground one.

We used to listen to the first Smiths album all the time during my year at college. Well, not ALL the time, but there were days when you suspected that the entire student population of Britain had decamped to college carrying nothing more than an optimistic packet of three, a couple of hip T-shirts and the first Smiths LP.

During the first few months I went round visiting some of my old school friends at their various universities and they all had The Smiths album as well, except, ironically, my best mate from sixth form Steve Cooke, who studied on The Smiths' home turf in Manchester. Instead, Steve – previously, and, it turns out, still to this day, a massive fan of Brian Setzer's Stray Cats – had discovered somebody called Indians In Moscow and the anecdotally unchallenged Martin Stephenson & The Daintees, who had both played at his local Student Union in the first term. Bands used to do brilliantly on the college circuit in the autumn because everywhere they went there was a cheap beer promotion.

Elsewhere, though, it was The Smiths and New Order all the way. When I visited Sheffield, a friend told me that New Order's 'Blue Monday' was the in tune to get laid to and you could tell when someone was having sex because it would start blaring through the corridors of his halls of residence. That's when all the big alternative bands of the time started to make sense. New Order (getting laid). The Smiths (not getting laid). Then came Billy Bragg (politics) and a year later The Pogues (drinking), and that was your University Of Life soundtrack pretty much sorted. Everyone was allowed their own maverick variations, but no college jukebox could survive without the Big Four.

And so some of the ground that had been lost in the charts after the demise of punk and 2 tone started to be reclaimed. I'm sure it wasn't just students who were buying the alternative music of the time – most of them, like me, were probably taping it off the radio or other friends – but the student dollar was an important factor in pop's make-up.

You can tell an incredible amount about who's in and who's out of fashion by inspecting the posters that adorn the walls of halls of residence around the country. It stands to reason. First-year freshers faced with four blank walls either bring or buy a selection of posters to wallpaper their rooms at the start of term (have you ever been to a university that didn't have a man come round once a week selling huge posters in the sports hall?).

I've often pondered whether there is a relationship between the three-year student cycle and the rise and fall of various alternative groups. Because if you take a look at some of the most student-friendly bands, they appear in the first year, reach their peak in the second and then after three years they start to fade. Musical scenes have been known to suffer the same fate.

Take Britpop, for instance. If your average fresher arrived in the autumn of 1994 with their Oasis posters and championed the

Britpop bands through their three-year course… then by the spring of 1997 they're returning home and it's all over. No more cheap beer or bands. It's off to work, more responsibility and a huge loan to pay off. The gang of mates you used to go to gigs with has been broken up, and there might not be the money around to indulge in music or gigs anyway.

The bigger bands survive, but the rest – the ones who fail to make it past being another cult college group – seem to wither and disappear. It's just a thought.

I didn't have a three-year cycle. I was at college for only a year, but my musical taste was going haywire. I'd been through a stage of championing some good and not so good punk and indie bands because there didn't seem much else to do.

But via the Neurotics and my fanzine and gigs in London, I moved on from The Smiths, New Order, Orange Juice and The Psychedelic Furs and ended up somewhere else. In a world outside the charts. That's when I rediscovered John Peel.

CHAPTER 3

Getting Nowhere Fast

Unbelievably, it was my dad who introduced me to John Peel. Not literally, of course, because apart from them both watching Ipswich Town on a regular basis, there was very little chance of them ever bumping into each other. But one night, before going to bed, Dad was fiddling with the radio, flicking through the dial, when he chanced upon some extraordinary piece of folk music.

As his ears pricked up, he pushed the record button on his reel-to-reel player and caught the final three minutes of the song. At the end of it, the voice of Peel back announced the track – don't ask me what it was – and then went into a song from his session guests Siouxsie & The Banshees. Dad switched off.

A couple of nights later, under the cover of darkness in my bedroom, I found this John Peel character again. It was like discovering that life exists on a different planet. It took me a couple of months, sizing up possible career options, but eventually I decided I wanted to be John Peel. Well, not him, but I wanted to be Somebody Like Him: playing records he liked and then talking about them. And not just any records. Records that were *weird.*

The punk and new wave era boasted three very good radio shows. Peel, Mike Read – who was given the 8–10 p.m. slot on

Radio 1 to cater for the music spilling over from John's show – and Stuart Henry's *Street Heat* on Radio Luxembourg on a Saturday evening.

Of these, Read's slot was the most obvious forerunner of *The Evening Session*. Not just because of the timeslot, but also because Read played a slightly more accessible range of tunes to Peelie, which complemented John's two-hour magical mystery tour. After Read moved on to daytime, the evening show (no one had managed to find a name for it in those days) continued to exist, although it did have its ups and downs. Kid, now David, Jensen took over from Read, as the new wave began to fall apart. And then Richard Skinner arrived, slightly burdened by the lack of great alternative music at the time (which was probably why he played American band Green On Red on every show). Skinner was there when I rediscovered Radio 1 at college, but he was later followed by Janice Long, whose enthusiastic delivery became a big influence on the *Sesh* in the days of myself and Jo Whiley. Long was bubbly and effervescent and sounded like one of your mates. She was ageless and infectious and played Blyth Power and The Loft. I liked her.

But as my college exams drew ever closer, it was the return of Peel to my daily routine that made most of an impact. When I first listened to him I did what countless young fans of the time did. I listened at home, on school nights, with my headphones on and the bedroom light switched off so that my parents didn't know I was still awake. In return for this surreptitious set-up, he introduced me to all sorts of bands – groups whose records I still treasure even now. The Blue Orchids, The Fire Engines, Gang Of Four, Girls At Our Best, Silicon Teens. Even the early Adam & The Ants singles like 'Zerox' and 'Cartrouble'. You can still hear the influence of these early eighties independent bands today if you listen closely enough. What Peel had managed to do was to gather up the shrapnel from punk and make sense of it.

When I do radio shows now, I present them in the hope that somewhere along the line, one or more records I play will have a similar impact on a listener that Peel's playlist had on me in my teens. Mind you, listening to Peel caused untold misery as well.

What was the single most frustrating thing that could happen to an over-excitable, young and foolhardy pop fan? Back in those days it was hearing a record on the radio, saving up your money and then going to the shops on Saturday only to be told they hadn't got it. Not only did they not have it, but THEY'VE NEVER EVEN HEARD OF IT!

All that expectation, the thrill of the chase – and then at the end of it, nothing. As a last-ditch solution I used to send off for records from mail-order companies – in the same way that the internet is now taking up the slack left by poor shop distribution – but it wasn't the same. I always forgave Peel, though. After all, it wasn't his fault that Parrot Records didn't have 'Hold On' by Terminal (a record I spent years trying to track down, before buying a copy on the internet for £70). Anyway, who else were we going to turn to for advice on music? Peel was our personal tutor.

For many kids, me included, my bedroom was both my sanctuary and my own private world. And during homework hours Radio 1 became the soundtrack to it. The only people I would let in my bedroom – if they weren't looking for dirty clothes or bringing me cups of tea – were Mike Read and John Peel.

It's also partly his fault that I launched myself into that other bastion of bedroom culture – the fanzine. I used to have this *Peel Show* ritual where I'd write three-line reviews of some of the records he played. (Rather scarily I also had a marking system, which I later found out is exactly the same system that Peel used for years to denote his favourite tracks, although my star system only went up to three and his was out of ten. The Undertones' 'Teenage Kicks', mind you, got something like 36 stars.) It was from these three-line reviews that I got into writing for other fanzines, and then I launched my own.

A Pack Of Lies issue number one had 22 pages, a print run of 300 copies and came out while I was in the lower sixth at school. I sold it by post and at local gigs by groups like Colchester's Special Duties (whose singer Steve Green I still see occasionally in the crowd at Colchester United). By the time I got to college I was onto issue four and a print run of 400. I did the Neurotics, plus The Partisans, and filled the rest with reviews and waffle. At college, the National

Council for the Training of Journalists had put all of its students into digs – which meant I lived with a landlady in one of the estates near the swimming pool. She didn't mind my increasingly nocturnal lifestyle, but she did mind the rattle of the front-room ceiling as I tried stapling 100 copies of *Lies* in a single night in my bedroom upstairs. Once again, Peel was the noise in the background.

I got through college, but only just. I revised for my law exam on the Tube going to Hammersmith to see a band called Twisted Nerve, and when it came to the all-important shorthand exams, I failed three times before finally passing the required 100-word-a-minute barrier on the last day of term. I thought I'd never see Harlow again after that, but I was wrong.

After college I returned to Colne Engaine with its one shop, one pub and one village green – and mooched around the house plotting the future of my fanzine. I applied for a few jobs – partly to keep my parents happy – and was scarily offered an interview with a paper in Shrewsbury. But Shrewsbury was nowhere near London and London was where all the gigs were, so I blew the interview by saying that I might be unsettled living so far from home and went back to daytime TV and photocopying.

Then, out of the blue, Andy Griffin, a classmate from college, tipped me off about a job on the *Walthamstow Guardian* and within two weeks I was behind a desk sharpening my shorthand pencil. Not in Walthamstow – I'd missed that one – but on one of its sister papers, the *West Essex Gazette* in Loughton, a quietly anonymous suburb attached to the capital by nothing more than the Central Line. As junior reporter I got the golden weddings, the primary school picture captions and the High Street vox pops (the weekly feature where you stopped people in the street and asked them their views on proposals for a new bus stop by the fire station).

It's fair to say that I didn't settle in straight away. In fact, it's truer to say that as my three-month probation period came to an end, the editor expressed doubts about my ability and promptly gave me a fortnight in the central office to prove myself. In the end they relented and I went back to Loughton to write such memorable stories as 'Mum Gives Birth To Baby In Front Seat Of Mini' and the tale of disgraced Spurs goalkeeper Tony Parks. It's the latter which shows what an ingenious coward I used to be when it came to hard news.

Parks had appeared in court on a drink-driving charge at a time when magistrates were making examples of fallen footballers and handing out custodial sentences instead of fines. Parks escaped the rumoured prison term, but he couldn't escape the determined hacks of the local press.

Having written up the court case, the editor threw the story back in my face claiming that – quite rightly – the tabloids would beat us to it. "What I want you to do, Steve, is phone him up and ask him about his marriage and whether he's got a drink problem."

On balance, I didn't much fancy the idea of tackling a six-foot goalkeeper with claims that his personal life had driven him to ruin, but given my precarious position on the paper I had to show some willing. I found his number and made the call. I let the phone ring twice, put the receiver down with lightning speed, and then announced, "He's not in." This was on Friday. Our deadline day was Wednesday. I repeated this process on Monday and Tuesday and then it came to press day.

"Give him one last go," the chief reporter sighed.

By now I was so confident that he'd gone abroad – or was staying with friends – until the fuss had died down that I let the phone ring four times. And then he answered it. "Erm, it's Steve Lamacq from the *West Essex Gazette*. I wonder if you could spare me five minutes…"

Parks said this was fine. And I set off looking for a way of avoiding all talk of marriage and booze. If I could just get him to say something like "I am not the bad boy of soccer" that would be OK. The phone call seemed to go on for hours, but after what was probably 15 minutes of unadulterated pussyfooting, I gave it one last shot at goal. "Well, thanks, Tony, and I just wondered… a lot of local kids look up to you as their hero… so do you have any message for them now?"

"Um, yes," Parks considered. "I'd just like to say I'm not the bad boy of soccer."

THANKSVERYMUCHGOODBYE.

Sensing that maybe hard news wasn't my forte, I was moved again, this time to the sports desk at the *Harlow Gazette*. This suited me fine. I was living back at my old landlady's and covering local soccer matches on a Saturday, so I got Fridays off to go record shopping. By now I'd discovered a terrific little shop in Walthamstow, the wonderfully named Ugly Child Records. I'd also struck up a relationship with a girl who didn't mind too much that I'd disappear for nights on end to staple fanzines or write incomprehensible reviews of bands I'd seen at the Hammersmith Clarendon. In fact, quite the contrary. Helen Mead was the music writer on the *Gazette*'s rival paper, the *Harlow Star*, so we were always going to gigs together and, if we argued about anything, it was usually over the relative merits of Half Man Half Biscuit versus Pop Will Eat Itself.

After a year the *Gazette* promoted me to sports editor and gave me the pop music page to play with as well. Now you might not think that there was much pop music in Harlow in the early eighties, but let me tell you, Harlow – like many overlooked, small towns – was a hotbed of talent.

Real by Reel, The Sullivans, Some Other Day, The Tender Trap, Austin's Shirts, Paul Howard & Joe Clack, Blue Summer, The Pressure (later The Internationalists), The Hermit Crabs, the hippy group whose name I can't remember… ring any bells yet? No? Well, I suppose that's the point.

There are hundreds of local scenes in towns all over the country. Hundreds of bands from places like Portsmouth, or Doncaster, or Hastings – the sort of places that in rock'n'roll terms are forever overlooked and always out of fashion. One of their problems is that they have no pop heritage. They can't boast of previous successes (or if they can they're like Harlow, whose only Top 40 band at the time had been an early eighties group called Roman Holiday, a sort of genial alternative boy band with a penchant for wearing sailors' caps).

The other drawback with these places is that bands are often shockingly uninformed about the way the industry works and about the way you can cheat or shortcut your way to success. Unless you happen to have a retired member of a former Top 30 band living on your doorstep, or you've made a couple of good contacts in the industry, you can find yourself banging your head against a wall, until finally frustration forces you to give up.

But that didn't stop us banging on about the local groups at the time. I even ended up 'managing' one of them for about three months one summer. Some Other Day were a four-piece whose name unfortunately shortened to SOD. During my time at the helm, I spent £100 on a demo and endless hours inventing new ways of making them famous. "Listen everyone," I told them one night, in a specially convened battleplan meeting in the bar of Harlow Town Football Club. "We're not going to play bog-standard venues, we're going to play cinemas and theatres."

Apart from the ill-fated theatre tour (one date in Sudbury, which fell through), I tried every idea in the book. Worse still, I thought they were all original. I never once considered the fact that, just possibly, a million other bands had got there first. So we tried sending in the rave reviews from the local press (the ones that start "Local band The Hit are top of the pops with music fans" or something similar). We tried nice cassette sleeves and fancy biogs. And then, gaining in confidence – i.e. increasingly desperate – we went for the teaser campaign.

If there are any current or would-be pop managers reading this, whatever you do, don't try the teaser campaign. I'm so embarrassed by this one, I'm going to leave the room for five minutes.

Somewhere along the line, another local journalist had described Some Other Day as making "delightful trouser music". Nobody knew what this meant but we decided that 'trouser music' was the enigmatic, hit-making formula of the future. Before sending out the new demo, we drew up a hitlist of A&R people and journalists and sent them a single photocopied note which claimed: "Trouser music is coming." No mention of the band whatsoever, just the trouser music. That would get them thinking.

Next was a second photocopy – this time with the name of the group in bold at the bottom. Then we followed that a week later by sending the lucky few a pair of Action Man trousers. Clever, eh? Finally we unleashed the demo with an invitation to see trouser music in the flesh: Some Other Day at the Mean Fiddler in Harlesden.

Nobody turned up. Strike that. A coachload of fans from Harlow turned up, but the rest of the music industry remained unfathomably un-teased. Still, at least we didn't go as far as the interesting box.

Once a month when I was at Radio 1, I'd walk into the office to find a massive or oddly shaped box sitting on my chair. And as soon as I arrived, a small crowd gathered, initiating the following exchange.

"Go on, open it."

"I wouldn't get excited. It'll be a demo tape."

"Don't be silly. In that? Go on, open it."

First you had to get past the layers of gaffer tape. Then once inside, it was like a bran tub full of the foamy stuff you get with new electrical gear. And then somewhere at the bottom... there was a demo tape.

"Oh. Is that all?" somebody always muttered. "I thought it was going to be exciting."

Well, it could have been. It could have been the future of rock'n'roll or the reinvention of rap music or an illicit bootleg of some early Foo Fighters sessions! But it never was. I've had demos that have come in pizza cartons, boxes that once held electric kettles and toasters – and it's virtually never been exciting. I mean, I live in hope. How great would it be to appear on a programme in years to come, explaining how a band the size of U2 first sent you a tape in a wheelie-bin. And before you get any ideas – don't try it. I once wrote a piece for a musicians' magazine where I explained that the packaging of a demo has no bearing on whether I'll play it or not. "For all I know, the best ones will come wrapped in toilet paper," I concluded. You can probably guess the rest.

The interesting box concept, though rarer, still survives today, even though the mechanics of sending new music to radio stations has changed dramatically.

More commonly now, you'll receive an email with a link to a website or with an MP3 attached. It's clearly an easier option. The danger is, though, with hundreds of these missives a week, that it's much harder to make yours stand out (or harder for the journalist or DJ to spot the more inventively minded artists out there).

I'm amazed at how many groups send emails that simply read: "We are a band from X. This is our new track. We hope you can play it on the radio."

No information, no manifesto, no big picture (or any picture, in fact). I don't know what the internet equivalent of the pizza box is, but if someone finds it, I'll be sure to let you know.

CHAPTER 4

Mirror Star

Working with a band didn't make me rich, but it did give me my first real insight into what bands are like. How they function – and, to be honest, how they malfunction.

How every small bit of good news is a signal that "Yes, at last, we're on our way," and how every crumb of bad news means it's the end of the road before they've even started. Over the years I've seen it time and time again, and I've thanked my lucky stars that I never wanted to be in a band.

Oh, there was a time when I did, I suppose. Aged 10–15, I did the whole air guitar thing in my bedroom and if I got really carried away I probably imagined myself being photographed for a magazine, maybe. But I don't think there was much conviction to these daydreams. In this imaginary group I was always the bass player. Looking back, I suspect this indicates a certain ambivalence or lack of self-belief to start with. (Why wasn't I the singer or the lead guitarist, like most people are in their heads? Why? Because, realistically, I thought the bass would be easier to learn? And it struck me, from looking at pictures of bands, that as the bassist, you didn't have to be particularly good-looking or articulate to pick up your wage. All you had to do was play the bass as far down by your knees as possible and occasionally supply backing vocals to prove to the audience that you were still breathing.)

But then, at around 16, it struck me that being in a band wasn't a career I was either: a) capable of; or b) that interested in. It occurred to me that it was actually bloody hard work. And besides… I didn't have a bass guitar and I didn't look like Joy Division's Peter Hook, who was the coolest bass player on the planet. But I really wasn't that fussed, so before anyone trots out the line about journalists being frustrated musicians, think again. For all the writers who *have* tried and failed in bands before becoming critics, there are hundreds who never really gave it that much thought.

It's not the same for everyone, though. There is that scene in *Withnail and I* when Richard Griffiths as Uncle Monty is recalling his failed acting career. Mournfully and theatrically he finishes by saying: "It is the most shattering experience of a young man's life when he wakes one morning and says to himself: 'I will never play the Dane.' When that moment comes, one's ambition ceases."

Sometimes I imagine would-be pop stars going through the same trauma. Only it's not playing the Dane. In past times it would have been playing *Top Of The Pops*, or these days *Later…*, or maybe headlining Wembley Arena or even being chased by screaming Californian groupies through the corridors of a five-star hotel. I'm sure there are a variety of fantasies that musicians had, or still have.

But luckily I managed to sidestep them. I think because I'd studied pop stars (what they looked like and the way they talked), I knew that I wasn't one of them. I did need an escapist dream, but it wasn't this one. I did finally buy a bass guitar when I was 18 – £35 including the case through a friend in a Colchester band called The Mysterie Boys – but I've never stood on stage with it. Crazily, four or five bands over the years have asked if I'd guest with them, but I've turned the offer down every time. Still, I did teach myself most of the Ramones' back catalogue and 'Clean Sheets' by Descendents, so I'm happy enough. And I do follow the bass-playing rules laid down by Hook and the punk movement.

It's an easy litmus test of how good a group is: the lower the bassist's guitar, the better the band. Level 42, UB40 – too high, no good. Not for me. The Ramones, New Order, the Mary Chain – bass by their ankles, good. I thank you.

So I didn't ever exist in the dreamworld that new bands live in. And I've never had to book a rehearsal room or sack a drummer, or wince when the dopey guitarist tries to shoehorn an AC/DC solo into one of my songs. But being a critic, you can live a vicarious lifestyle, standing on the edge of all these bands and watching them going through the whole process.

For a start there's an awful lot to practise. How to stand. How to walk. What to say in interviews. What not to let your drummer say in interviews. Then there's the whole problem with your signature. Even I'll own up to this one. I spent days once as a teenager practising new signatures, because my regular run-of-the-mill chequebook one looked like the creation of a two-year-old with a blunt crayon. So I invented new ones (dozens of them) before finally deciding on the one I use now.

I know I'm generalising here, but 90 per cent of young guitar bands live a colourful and romantic Walter Mitty world. Everything, when a group forms, is a step closer to fame. The first rehearsal, the first two new songs... then, the first gig. Then you get to make a demo – possibly in a real recording studio.

Next it's a support slot to someone semi-famous, then the first big gig in London or Manchester or Glasgow or wherever. There's mentions in the local press or an enthusiastic blog or two – and if you're lucky your first radio play or upward blip in streaming figures on Spotify or similar.

And this is where bands go in separate directions. The lucky (or in some cases hard-grafting) ones get a break and are on their way to the Top 40, festival headlining status and tours of Japan. The unlucky ones, the ones who aren't very good, or don't happen to be in the right place at the right time, suddenly discover that the world hasn't been waiting for them. And I know, especially these days, that not all artists are possessed by a need to be big time, that there are hundreds of different levels of success that have more do with artistry or live engagement than top-line chart sales.

You can find your niche in a genre, or be big in Germany, and that's enough. Why wouldn't it be? But back in the eighties and nineties, and for the teenagers who still now see their name outside Brixton Academy or the image of themselves being flown in for the MTV Awards, there is a point when, more often than not, reality bites.

It might be a bad gig, or a scathing review, or just the general, unfeeling apathy of the general public towards their latest experimental masterpiece. It could just be the onset of jealousy as you see all those bands who are quite patently not as good as you receiving all the acclaim and getting all the attention. But sooner or later, it's time to concede defeat and pack it in.

And I don't know what's worse here. Would you rather have got quite close to fame (a record deal, a couple of tours and a minor hit maybe, or an award nomination), or would you rather have called it a day before having the rock'n'roll lifestyle dangled in front of you, and then cruelly snatched away again as your follow-up album gets two out of ten in a magazine review? Whichever. There has to be a day when you realise it's never going to happen, doesn't there?

For some musicians this is harder to face than for others. That's why there are so many ex bands in existence (featuring former members of formerly quite good groups who are simply hooked on the lifestyle and obsessed by the dream).

And groups who just refuse to give up. Bands who've been kicking around for years and have never given up hope that one day their break will come. The demos regularly turn up at 6 Music from people who are still pursuing a vision of sell-out gigs in stadiums, or, on a less grand scale, a place at the top of the bill of the second stage at their local boutique festival.

And sadly a lot of them aren't very good. For them that day will never come. And I don't exactly know what I feel about this. I admire the conviction and self-belief (in the same way that I feel some sympathy for the man who's invested his life savings in an invention, which is promptly shot to pieces in two minutes on *Dragons' Den*). But maybe it wasn't a good idea. Maybe they should have put the guitar down a decade ago, or simply carried on playing for fun as lots of people do, spared the nagging thought that if only they could get the right manager or the elusive radio station playlist, everything would fall into place.

So for all the terrific times I would have had, through doing gigs, and telling my mum I'd soon be on *Top Of The Pops*, I'm happy enough to eschew the allure of the pop business. I just don't think I could have coped with being so near, and yet so far.

CHAPTER 5

Whenever I'm Gone

Everyone has a band that they think should have been massive, but who never were. They could be mates from your local town, or a group signed to a major record label. It doesn't matter. They were great – and the rest of the world just didn't see it. Over the years I've acquired about 100 of these bands. But if I had to pick just the one, then it's The Prisoners.

I'd put my fanzine on hold for a year while concentrating on the pop page of the *Harlow Gazette* (a page that, in the tradition of local paper youth music, had the cringeworthy title 'Our Generation'). But *A Pack Of Lies* returned with three issues in quick succession, starting with number eight, which was a comeback special featuring lots of incomprehensible reviews. But it was good to be back. I'm not sure if it was a particularly good time for fanzines, but through the eighties many of the future music press writers cut their teeth in the underground world of photocopy machines and High Street print shops.

The peak of it for me was when a bunch of us set up a fanzine stall in London's Brockwell Park, where the GLC was staging a free outdoor gig. (The Damned played, I think, and probably Aswad. It's a bit of a haze because the GLC was always putting on gigs around the time of the Miners' Strike and the Wapping Dispute. I think that's why a certain age group of Londoners were always so supportive of former GLC leader Ken Livingstone. They associate him with cheap Tube fares and being able to see The Smiths and The Redskins for free on the South Bank.)

Our stall was on a walkway between the two live music stages and was run by Dave Hurt (*Love and Molotov Cocktails* fanzine), Richard Cool Notes and his mate, me and future editor of *Loaded* magazine James Brown. Brown was always the most entertaining. Midway through the afternoon, he stopped two passing policemen and, in a display of salesmanship that was second to none, flogged them not only a copy of his own fanzine, *Attack On Bzag* – a riotous mix of pop and politics – but one of mine as well.

That was the thing about being a fanzine editor – it made you part of a little community with a spirit all of its own. Sure there was a certain amount of cliquishness and rivalry around – but between them, the fanzines and bedroom indie labels formed a small pocket of resistance to the generally bland mainstream of the time.

Pre-internet days, we swapped letters and cassettes and phone calls and you didn't rely on the press to tell you what was going on, because each week someone you knew or had just met would introduce you to a new band or great record. Through *A Pack Of Lies* I met Andy Peart, who was behind the excellent *So What* fanzine; and through Andy I met Leigh Heggarty from a band called The Price (though these days he's now the guitarist in Ruts DC). And through Leigh I found The Prisoners.

Andy and Leigh have introduced me to a lot of music over the years, but it's The Prisoners that I really owe them for. They couldn't have suggested a better band if they'd gone through some kind of Dateline selection process matching me to my perfect partner. The Prisoners were, without doubt, the most sullen, angry and heart-breaking four-piece I'd ever heard. They scowled for Britain. One evening we managed to get into the soundcheck of their gig at Uxbridge University and cheerfully waved at them as they arrived. They completely blanked us.

If that sounds masochistic, then doesn't everyone go through a stage of loving someone who behaves appallingly to them? What was that the Buzzcocks said about falling in love with someone you shouldn't have fallen in love with? Their names were Graham Day,

Jamie Taylor, Allan Crockford and Johnny Symons. And they had a song called 'Melanie'.

And I'm not alone in this. Although they received very little press coverage at the time, several writers who ended up in the music press in the nineties revered them – as did various bands, including The Charlatans and Inspiral Carpets. The two girls from the band Lush were even at some of the same Prisoners gigs I was at, long before I'd ever met them.

There are several Prisoners albums to choose from, if you want to hear what they were like – though personally I'd go for the third LP, *The Last Fourfathers*. It's got some of the saddest, some of the most bitter and some of the most vitriolic songs I think I own.

There are probably many reasons why their career never truly got off the ground. Despite emerging from the fleetingly talked-about Medway scene, they weren't the hippest new band around. The music papers were having a mid-eighties identity crisis (leading up to the invention of the C86 movement on the one hand and grebo on the other). And The Prisoners' faces didn't fit. You could even make a case that they were slightly retro-sounding even then.

But they did OK for a time. They were filmed live for the cult TV show *The Tube*, they toured the UK and were Big In Europe. And after *The Last Fourfathers*, they finally signed to a bigger label – the quirky Stiff Records, which had grown out of the pub-rock and punk scenes of the late seventies. It would have probably been a good move, had it not been for the fact that Stiff was just about to hit financial strife. And, according to the band, the A&R staff kept leaning on them to clean up their sound and go for the Big Hit Single. A fourth album, *In From The Cold*, was preceded by a reworking of 'Whenever I'm Gone' (rerecorded from *The Last Fourfathers*) as the potential Top 40 chartbuster. I dashed off to Ugly Child to buy it on the day of release, but it steadfastly refused to chart and the situation between band and label worsened.

Reaching the end of their tether, the band arranged two farewell gigs in London. The first was at the Fulham Greyhound, which I couldn't go to for some reason. But I bought a ticket for the second one at the legendary 100 Club in Oxford Street. They played out of their skins on the night. They always played like the world was ending round their ankles – but at the 100 Club they were on fire. All the anger, all the venom, all the frustration that had built up inside them… it all came out. They even played two new songs, including one called 'Pop Star Party' which was dedicated to Stiff. (There is a rarities compilation that features a demo of this track. Halfway through, it stops and there's a five-second gap. In Day's sleeve notes, he explains that there's where the master tape snapped as they were trying to wrestle the tapes out of the hands of the label.)

Whatever other demons they were wrestling with at the 100 Club, they must have been out of their trees as well. By the time they launched into the final song of the encore, they were passing round a bottle of Jack Daniels. Meanwhile, Day, during an elongated instrumental middle section, started announcing their future career plans: "On drums, Johnny 'I'm going back to college' Symons."

After it was all, finally, over, Jamie Taylor staggered off stage and – trying hard to focus – walked through the crowd to a corner of the club. Swaying slightly, he arranged four chairs in a row, and then lay down on them… and promptly fell asleep. Before leaving, Leigh and I went and just stared at him.

"What a man," said Leigh.

Scarily, it was like paying your respects to someone who had passed away. I was going to say that he might still be there now for all I know, but Taylor rose again. Within a year he was back with the James Taylor Quartet. Crockford joined him on bass for a while, but soon departed.

There were rumours that none of them got on very well. But Crockford and Day returned again with a new band, The Prime Movers – and in the mid-nineties they finally relented and reformed The Prisoners, releasing a single and playing several dates. We all went along, despite the nagging doubts that it wouldn't be the same; that they would have mellowed or made peace with the world. But, to my immense delight, they hadn't. Fuck me, it was still The Prisoners.

CHAPTER 6

Pump Up The Volume

Somewhere in the files of *Melody Maker* there are a couple of issues from 1985 that feature live reviews by a girl called Julie. That's me.

Well, desperate measures for desperate times and all that… But I came to the conclusion that having written a fanzine, the next step in championing new bands was to write for the music press. So, like scores of would-be journalists before me, I sent in a couple of unsolicited reviews and waited for them to appear in print. They never did.

Years later I found that the main papers hardly ever ran unsolicited work, but at the time I was hopelessly ill-informed and carried on my letter-writing campaign for months. Matters became worse when I read an article about how Garry Bushell, the former *Sounds* journalist turned tabloid columnist, had got his break. Allegedly he'd been to see ten gigs in ten consecutive nights and reviewed all ten, a day at a time. Every morning the reviews editor arrived and opened his post – there was another review from Gaz.

So I tried this. At the end of the ten days (and nights) I phoned the live desk and the weary section editor Barry McIlhenny said yes, he'd read them, and yes, if a trial review came along for me to do, he'd phone me. He never did. I actually thought I'd driven him over the edge because, checking in the staff box – which was the list of the paper's contributors – a month later, his name had vanished.

The upside of this was that there was new guy in charge who wouldn't recognise my style of writing. He might even like it. But wait. First I found a band that the paper weren't covering – in this case Action Pact – and then I jazzed up the writing a little and signed it off with a girl's name.

A fortnight later, standing in a newsagent, having bunked off work for half an hour, I opened the *MM* and the review was in. I slowly closed the paper… then opened it again. It was still there. I'd arrived. They hadn't even changed much of the copy. I sent them a second review, this time of the Neurotics, and that went in as well. Then a third… which didn't.

Of course, I should have phoned them – or got a girl to phone on my behalf, to keep up the ruse – but I thought all I had to do was wait a couple of weeks and write in under my real name and everything would be fine. Again, it wasn't.

Because when I went back to being Steve Lamacq they went back to ignoring me, and I gave up. Even worse, I arrived home one night to find my landlady writing 'Not known at this address' on the cheque they'd sent Julie for her efforts. Actually, she might as well have sent it back.

Have you ever tried convincing the Co-op Bank that a cheque with a girl's name on it is really for the skinny young man standing in front of them?

There had to be an easier route than this.

It was my then girlfriend Helen who got the first break. Having had a few reviews printed in *Smash Hits*, she landed the job of live reviews editor at the *New Musical Express*, while I shambled around trying to work out my next move. It's blindingly obvious now. I should probably have attempted to twist her arm, or emotionally blackmail her into giving me some reviews to do. But at the time the thought never crossed my mind. I think I was desperate to prove myself on my own (either that or I was simply too proud or too dumb to come up with the idea). So I hung around on the periphery of the press and waited for the next vacancy.

Eventually there was not one but two job ads in the old weekly music papers in one week. The first was in *Sounds*, the second in the *NME*: 'Subeditor wanted'. This was it. Unbelievably, having fired off the two CVs, enclosing a recent issue of *A Pack Of Lies*, I was offered interviews by both.

Now, I wouldn't normally have known anything about music paper editors, but I remembered Alan Lewis's name from the old staff boxes in *Sounds* around the glory days of the early eighties. Lewis was now *NME* editor, recently installed to help stabilise the paper, whose sales had fallen beneath the magic 100,000 target each week. I remember precisely nothing about the interview apart from the fact that I wore a suit and I wished I hadn't and that Jam biographer and *NME* staff writer Paolo Hewitt passed me by the lift.

Over at *Sounds*, then based in the austere Greater London House near Mornington Crescent Tube station, Tony Stewart made more of an impression because he hit me with a barrage of difficult questions about pop music boundaries and defining genres. Even then, though, I had a few half-cock theories which I trolled out, mixed up with a bit of punk rock spite, which seemed to do the trick. It was Stewart's closing question that took me most by surprise: "Are you going for the *NME* job?" Now what was I supposed to say to this? "No, I am 100 per cent *Sounds* through and through and I would not sully the good name of your paper by setting foot behind enemy lines."

The way it came out was: "Um, yeah, but I haven't heard anything..."

A day later *NME* secretary Karen Walter phoned and invited me for a day-long trial in the subs room. And then everything went haywire. I heard via my girlfriend that a senior member of the writing staff had been fired – and that the day of my trial coincided with a day of possible strike action over claims of unfair dismissal.

"Well, that's just typical," I harrumphed. "I finally get a break at *NME* and I can't go, because I can't cross a picket line." Only I think I used more expletives than that, and I may well have had a couple of drinks to soften the blow.

In the end, the strike didn't happen. But the threat of it was still hanging in the air as I arrived in the secretary's office for a start time of 10.30 a.m. Lewis looked harassed and troubled and took me to one side. "Day's trial, oh yes. Right, erm, well, I've got one or two things to sort out, and erm…" (At this point he paused and looked distractedly in the direction of the editorial room.) Finally, turning back, he added: "So, erm. Well, look, do you want the job?"

"Well, yeah."

"OK, good. See Karen on the way out and let her know how much notice you have to work, and when you can start. Welcome aboard."

Two minutes later I was back out in New Oxford Street. Slightly stunned.

The first year at the *NME* was like an apprenticeship. There was a lot to learn about the music industry and the media. But then again, the music industry had a lot to learn about itself. Change was in the air.

The first *NME* I ever worked on had Public Enemy on the cover. A month later the front page was headlined: 'HOLD AND STORE: Coldcut, MARRS And The Art Of Sampling.' Technology was starting to infuse dance music with new ideas – and although the Christmas cover that year still featured old troopers like New Order and U2, you could feel the growing appetite among bands and fans to move on. It would take another year of slow progress before anything much blossomed, but the seeds of the nineties were already being planted.

On a personal note, I had a bumpy first few months at *NME*. What am I saying? I had a bizarre first three days. On day two I stood quivering at the gents urinals next to Mark E Smith from The Fall. On day three, long-standing skinhead writer Steven Wells stomped into the subs room and slammed a heap of copy down on the desk in front of me, while barking: "YOU! NEW BOY! Who are you then?"

Bloody hell. It was like *Tom Brown's Schooldays*. Any second now, this mad ranting poet turned music scribe – this muscley ball of suppressed energy – is going to put my head down the toilets. Only he didn't, and like a lot of the staff, Swells' bark was worse than his bite. I'd just started to find my feet when I had the nightmare week from hell. First, I split up with the Harlow girlfriend – in particularly painful circumstances. She decided to give me the elbow in favour of a freelancer at *NME*. (Would you like to know that this happened the week after Valentine's Day?) Two days after we had the break-up conversation in the pub, Alan Lewis called me into his office, and for the second time in consecutive jobs, I had my three-month trial period extended because I wasn't meeting the paper's standards.

Among their duties, as well as writing headlines and captions, subeditors are responsible for checking the spelling in features and reviews. It hadn't taken Alan that long to tumble that I couldn't spell – and they extended my trial for another month. Quite how I was going to learn to spell in that time I couldn't work out, but I ran around looking extra enthusiastic for the next month and put in all the hours I could, and Alan took pity on me, for which I will be eternally grateful.

But it was a horror week that ended with me being virtually scraped off the floor by reviews editor Alan Jackson, who bought me beer and chips and told me not to worry, and that there were plenty more fish in the sea. He put me up for the night and gave me a pep talk and sent me on my way. It was a terrific act of kindness I've never forgotten.

And having come through that, I was handed the biggest prize of my *NME* career to date. They let me loose on the singles page.

The *NME* singles page was a big deal on many levels. Press officers were desperate for their records to get a good review, especially at the start of a campaign, so there was a whiff of power around you the week you did the singles. And it gave the writer a WHOLE PAGE to play with. A whole page to show off your insane opinions and unburden yourself of your current prejudices. Not to mention, for the freelance writer, a decent cheque at the end of it and a lot of free records.

I did scores of singles over the years, but I remember the first one more vividly than most. There was the initial excitement of opening all the mailers marked 'Singles Reviews' – and then the crushing realisation that it was going to take you hours to listen to them all, and most of them would be rubbish. Then, like homework, you'd put off the actual writing until the last moment, and end up finishing at 3 a.m.

So, think about this, bands, because if your record ever had a good kicking in the press, the chances were that the review was written at the end of the writer's tether at 2 a.m. (approximately two hours after his supply of lager and cigarettes had run out).

But the first singles page came in an issue which revealed a lot about alternative pop culture in 1988. Morrissey was on the cover talking about the collapse of The Smiths and the arrival of his solo LP, *Suedehead*. Inside there were pieces on The Fall, The Triffids and Ennio Morricone – plus a full page ad for Sting's new single 'Englishman In New York'. The news pages included stories on Billy Bragg, Madness reforming and Mozzer again. It looks stale and lifeless now and tied to the past – though at least by this point the paper had dropped its weekly strapline, which exclaimed 'Over 25 albums reviewed inside' (a sign of the times – these days magazines boast of 25 *pages* of reviews, not 25 albums).

There were some specks of light, though: a feature on Fon Studios, a rabid and enthusiastic critic of Dub Sex, and a lead album review for *Justified Ancients Of Mu Mu*. For my part, I weighed in with a mixed bag of mainly dull records (The Sugarcubes: 'Radically remixed, devastatingly soporific' – I bet that had them quaking in their pixie boots, eh?). The one bright spark was the Single Of The Week. It arrived just before the deadline, and I knew nothing about it – save for the press release, which was a bunch of made-up old tosh anyway – but the best single of the week was 'Beat Dis' by Bomb The Bass. It was a sign of things to come.

For the following year I kept my head down in the subs room, wrote the occasional article or review, and went to more gigs. Then I got another lucky break. Denis Campbell left his post as assistant news editor and I replaced him as second in command to news editor Terry Staunton. Out of the subs room, and on to the news desk. I was a proper journalist again.

Terry taught me how to fill in an expenses sheet. And at the start of my second week, the two Karens from the Beggars Banquet press office took us out to lunch. For a fortnight I was so happy, I barely knew what to do with myself. Then it was time to start the crusade.

CHAPTER 7

Severe Attack Of The Truth

I've been lucky over the years to have a series of great allies: people who've stood up for me or supported me, or, in some instances, simply shared my own, peculiar vision of what pop music should be; people who've had my back at work or people I've been able to turn to in a crisis.

There have been some good bosses, some hard-working and intuitive editors and producers; and there have been my fellow journalists, one or two of whom are probably as dysfunctional in some ways as I am – not least the man who would go on to be my greatest ally at the *NME*: Simon Williams.

After work at the *Harlow Gazette* on a Monday, I used to drive into London to Dingwalls in Camden. Dingwalls ran a regular Monday-night club called Panic Station, which used to showcase some of the best indie and alternative bands around at the time. Not only that, but it was a good place to sell fanzines. If you got there early enough you could offload up to 30 copies in a night, and have enough money to keep you in cider and chips till the end of the week.

The Dingwalls crowd had a strange quirk, though. No matter how much they were into the bands and the music, they'd only ever buy *one* fanzine a night. So if you arrived late and found another magazine had already done the rounds, well, that was that. You might as well go and impale yourself on a mic stand.

Sure enough, I was late the night I met Simon. My heart sank as I walked into the venue and, en route to the bar, passed various floppy-haired indie kids all flicking through a 'zine called *Jump Away*. That was my drink budget up the creek for the week. I bumped into Williams later on and we introduced ourselves to each other and swapped fanzines (he had only two left – I had a carrier bag heaving with copies).

I'm sure we must have seen each other around at gigs after that, but our friendship didn't really start to form until after he'd packed in his job as shelf-stacker at Sainsbury's and began freelancing for *NME*. Having come from a similar fanzine background, we were both imbued with the same desire to storm the barricades.

By 1989 we'd formed an unlikely rebel alliance at *NME*. We used to have a war office in the Stamford Arms pub next to IPC every Tuesday lunchtime and we'd go to gigs at the Kentish Town Bull and Gate and Camden Falcon every week. Every time we had a review cut or a feature turned down we'd retire to the pub and rant and vent. We were the Blues Brothers of Indie. We were on a mission.

Or, in Simon's case, he reviewed The Mission.

In 1989 God gave us Madchester and the continuing rise of rave culture. But he gave us quite a lot else too. The indie label scene was beginning to flourish again after an awful two years and the live circuit suddenly began to fill up with rabid new bands who could recite the name of every service station between London, Manchester and Glasgow.

It definitely felt like 1989 was the end of something, but what was it? It wasn't just the end of the decade; it felt like it should be the end for drab old middle-of-the-road alternative music as well. Many of the bands that would shake up the nineties were either just beginning to break through or lying in wait in the shadows.

And, in the meantime, what were Simon and I doing? Well, caught up in fanzine culture and reeking of beer, we were the self-appointed A&R scouts of the *NME*. In the making of this book, we both checked our old diaries and we were out all the time. I'm not sure about Simon, but my own selection process couldn't have been that consistent, because there are bands there who I have no recollection of. For instance, who were Kiev Exocet (George Robey, January 4), or Trashcan Soul (Bull and Gate, January 13), The Toll (100 Club, March 13), Kid Glad Glove (Walthamstow Royal Standard, August 1 – the Royal Standard?!!!), Fat Controllers (Robey, August 8) or Bad Caesar (Marquee, October 9)?

There must have been reasons for seeing these groups. It's not like we just selected bands randomly from the *Gig Guide*, or wandered the streets of London until we heard the noise of rock guitars emanating from inside a pub. There were good gigs, of course, as well as the bad ones.

And then there was the most poorly attended gig I've ever been to. That dubious honour falls to a group called Last Party, who had just recorded a John Peel session and had released an acerbic and atmospheric single called 'Die In A Spy Ring'. The venue for the gig was a bit off the beaten track – the New Pegasus in Stoke Newington – but Simon and I decided to go anyway.

Now there could be several reasons why this gig was so underpopulated: lack of advertising; it was a drab Tuesday night; the Pegasus wasn't exactly well served by public transport. But by the time we arrived, the man on the door looked like he had given up the will to live. The sight of two punters arriving appeared to cheer him up momentarily – but when we announced we were on the guest list, he went back to his emotional nosedive.

So we walked in, and that was when it hit us. We were the ONLY people there. No, tell a lie, there was a girl behind the bar. But apart from her, the promoter on the door and us… that was it. About ten minutes before the band came on, a further lonely soul – a young indie chap who had heard the band on Peel – arrived, AND PAID. But that was the crowd. A total of three people and two staff.

When the group arrived, Simon, the indie bloke and I arranged three chairs in front of the stage and cheered the Party on. When they finished we made them do an encore.

To their credit, the band took it all in good heart. (Were they used to playing to three people? Was it, in fact, a good night for them?)

Their big-hearted singer – also, we found out, called Simon – came off stage and bought the entire audience a drink.

It wasn't all bad, though. Through 1989 we brought in a series of bands who would go on to have a measure of success in the next few years. Simon uncovered Lush, I stumbled across Ride, who were supporting a Brighton band called The Popguns at the Falcon, then there was The Family Cat, Inspiral Carpets, Carter The Unstoppable Sex Machine, Senseless Things, Snuff and Mega City Four.

The Megas held a particular place in our hearts, for all sorts of reasons. We liked the music and Wiz's lyrics (there was a time when I thought the first MC4 album said more about my life than any other single record). We liked the fact that they'd play anytime, anyplace, anywhere; and that this was an important factor in the revival of small club gigs around the country. And we liked the lack of posturing, pretentiousness and pop star nonsense.

But underlying all this, I think we used the Megas as a metaphor for our position at *NME*. They were outsiders, and unfashionable, and if they wanted to make something happen, they had to get out there and do it for themselves.

I saw the Megas an awful lot in 1989 (I daren't actually add up all the mentions in the diary). But they provided a lifeline at times. I suppose if I'm really honest I used the Megas to haul me clear of the two-day depressions I went through for a couple of months when I began to feel that life – post break-up and without a feature commission in weeks – was starting to look bleak.

There is one batch of dates, though, that I remember more vividly than any others. I had a week off, so with nothing else to do, I drove up to see them play at Norwich Arts Centre. Having nowhere to stay afterwards – money was tight and the Megas had probably cornered the market in kipping on people's floors – I tried sleeping in the car again, in a nearby car park. At about 2 a.m. there was a loud tapping on the window. And sure enough it was the police come to arrest me.

"Are you the owner of this car?"

"Yes. Well, no. It's my dad's. I've borrowed it."

"Can you prove that?"

What, at 2 a.m.? "Look, is there a problem?"

"We've had a lot of trouble with vagrants breaking into cars in this area and sleeping in them and we believe that…"

Yes, they think I'm a vagrant. They wouldn't go away. Finally, after I'd bored them silly with stories about Mega City Four and they'd checked the vehicle records, they moped off looking exceedingly disappointed ("Thought we had one there…").

The next day, freezing cold and on four hours' sleep, I drove further north to Hull to see the Megas again at the Hull Adelphi (one of the UK's longest-running grassroots venues – a converted terraced house on the outskirts of the city), where they were on terrific form and entirely in their element. And then the next day it was on to Birmingham, where I had some work to do. Even though it was officially my week off, I was down to review The Beautiful South on their first UK tour at the Irish Centre. First, though, I had to meet their press officer – and possibly members of the band – at a hotel in the city centre.

I walked up the steps to the entrance, where a man in a top hat stopped me.

"I'm sorry, sir, you can't go in there looking like that."

"Pardon?"

"You can't go in there looking like that," he said again, with his arm barring my way and his eyes looking straight over my head.

"I'm a resident. Well, I will be if I get in. I'm meeting people in there. Look, really. I'm not a vagrant!"

"Sorry sir."

Any suggestions? Help at this point? The penguin waddled off and then returned two minutes later.

"You may use the tradesmen's entrance. It's round the back. Take the lift to reception."

And that's how bad you could look after two days on tour with Mega City Four.

Despite all these sorties round the country, I think I only went to Manchester twice around this time. But Manchester was where it was all happening at the end of the eighties. By the start of 1989,

Happy Mondays were in the news every week. And in the same way that DJs started spending their summers commuting back and forth to Ibiza, a growing number of industry folk started spending their weekends in the north of England.

At the beginning of the year I don't think many of us knew why they were going (after all, they'd return a couple of days later saying they'd had a great time, but they looked bloody awful, as if they'd slept on a park bench, when, of course, they simply hadn't slept at all). And they'd started talking in that funny way, where your intonation goes up at the end of a sentence. What was that all about? I don't think it's an understatement to say that the Manchester bug – or even Manchester's real influence on latter-day pop – didn't entirely make much sense to me at the time. That is until I went on the road with, of all the unlikely messiahs, My Bloody Valentine.

It was a live page feature for the *NME*, taking in two nights of the tour – the first at Nottingham Trent Poly and the second at Manchester University. Both gigs were good but it was the second night, in Manchester, that ended with the most eye-opening of experiences – at the Hacienda. If I hadn't fully seen the foundations of Madchester before then, a lot of pieces suddenly fell into place that night.

But let's get My Bloody Valentine out of the way first. MBV have their own, very definite, place in the history of alternative music in this country. Born around the time of the cutesy C86 movement, they grew from a floppy-fringed fey pop band into a monstrous-sounding rock group. One whose experiments with sound and structure were possibly among the few things we had in Britain that would stand up against the likes of Sonic Youth's serrated-edged rock in the States. That was my angle anyway. My Bloody Valentine guitarist Kevin Shields was more modest and abstract in his view of the group. He was also one of the most softly spoken men I've ever met.

On the first night, conducting the interview in one of the Student Union offices at Trent Poly, Shields was so quiet that he was barely audible over the air conditioning, let alone the support band soundchecking. The whirr of the cassette recorder was louder than his voice. But he was thoughtful and courteous as well as pensive and reserved. The tour, meanwhile, was among the best they ever did. It was just as they had started including 10-, 12- or 14-minute versions of 'You Made Me Realise', which shouldered up against tracks from their *Isn't Anything* album. They were astonishingly loud, and lost in their own world on stage. They were mesmerising, they really were – and the Nottingham gig was in a room that looked like a sports hall. It shouldn't have worked at all, but it did.

The following night they did it all over again at Manchester Academy. But this time they had the added benefit of being the soundtrack to an increasingly surreal evening. I had travelled across from Nottingham with Jeff Barrett, part-time London promoter and press officer about town who handled the publicity for the bands on Creation Records. It was Barrett, strangely enough, who brought Madchester and Happy Mondays to London and got them to play at the Black Horse in Camden (he later went on to start Heavenly Records and work with the South's answer to the Mondays, Flowered Up). That night, after checking in, we met in the oddly ornate bar of the hotel where we were staying, just off the Oxford Road. It wasn't the weird decor that was the centre of attention, though; it was the people. Sprawled in the corner were various Creation folk, Manchester friends and hangers-on, and in the middle of this motley crew of 24-hour party people was Creation boss Alan McGee.

I'm not sure how many times I'd met Alan at this point – if indeed I'd met him at all – but with the ginger hair and gesticulating hands and wild eyes he was the most passionate man on the planet that night. Every sentence, every proclamation about his label or one of his bands ended with him saying, in his fired-up Glaswegian accent, "Do you see it, right, Steve... D'ya get it?" It was as if he was holding an idea in his hands – or a vision of the future, which included both his bands and his label, and you needed a key to unlock it. It was fascinating.

We moved on to the gig and MBV were out of this world again. There really were very few groups who could touch them at the time. (Note: I tried to come up with a list of my favourite ten gigs of all time for this book, but it was too big a task. By number seven I already had two MBV appearances, though – this one and the night they played in New York supported by Pavement and Superchunk.)

We finished off at the gig and left the indie noise behind. Then the increasingly large party hit the Hac.

It throbbed. Not just the building, but my head. Still reeling from the onslaught of My Bloody Valentine (and the consequent ringing in my ears caused by Kevin Shields' guitar), we walked into the Hacienda and I swear I just stood there blinking and throbbing.

So this was what all the fuss was about. It was rammed with people. And the speakers were spilling out a tune which had dressed itself in dayglo before going out for the night. If MBV had wiped out the treble in my hearing, then the Hac did for the bass. And I don't think I would remember so much about the night if one of our party hadn't had his first experience with E. Ecstasy was still in its infancy at the time. Or at least it hadn't made the sort of impact it would later have in the nineties as it began crossing over from the dance clubs into gigs and pubs and front-page stories on the tabloids.

All I knew was that it was supposed to make you dance all night like you had a Duracell battery stuck up your arse and it made you want to love everybody.

The trouble was that my E-virgin mate had got hold of one of the more powerful strains of E that were doing the rounds. After the initial boredom of waiting for the drug to take effect, he suddenly went very pale. Then he turned round and said: "Steve? Steve. The floor's turned to rubber." And then his legs turned to jelly. No Duracell battery at all. I sat him down in a quiet corner and fetched him a glass of water. Amazingly, within about five minutes he'd recovered and bunny-hopped off into the crowd.

It was a very odd night.

As one of the most talked-about clubs in Britain, the Hacienda also played a significant role in one of 1989's biggest stories: the arrival of The Stone Roses. Simon and I had first come across them through their 'Made Of Stone' single, which was one of our favourite records of the spring. Then there were all the stories that started filtering through from Manchester: about the graffiti campaign which had seen their name daubed over various public buildings, and how they were gigging all the time because their manager owned two of the city's venues.

A five-track album sampler cassette followed the single. And just before it went ballistic I saw them on tour at Uxbridge Brunel University. The students at Brunel never seemed to take notice of any of the gigs on their own doorstep, so despite the first wave of rave reviews in the press, the place was half-empty. You could walk right to the front, where there were about 20 early hardcore fans dancing in a small group. I took my mate Tall Graham and his girlfriend with me to show them the future of pop music. And although we'd never agreed on many bands before, we spent the entire car journey home round the M25 going on and on about them.

It was a good time to see them too, because it was the calm before the storm. Everything was about to come up roses for the Roses. Manchester was cool, club culture was beginning to entwine itself with rock music, and there in the middle of it all was this group who walked and talked like a real band. They had a solid masterplan as well. Just as the buzz surrounding them was reaching fever pitch, they staged a jam-packed showcase gig at the Hacienda. Their PR company took a handful of important journalists up to Manchester for the gig. And the Roses were showered with incredible reviews.

I saw them a couple of months later at the ICA in London on the night of a bus and Tube strike (so I must have been quite committed) and they were growing in confidence and swagger all the time.

I wrote the review in my head, while trying to get back to Liverpool Street station in time for the last train back to Harlow. The rest I scribbled on the back of a flyer the next morning on the way to work.

"There are three reasons why The Stone Roses are our favourite band of the month and why suddenly, hearteningly, they have their debut album tussling with the lame competition in the Top 30. First though a quick précis of tonight's gig. They go on late (nobody cares); they play the oddest ever ICA gig (nobody flinches) and perversely they tart around with the running order of the set and they don't do an encore."

The three reasons cited for their imminent rise to megastardom were: the songs; the fact that they'd got immeasurably better than "when we saw them at Central London Poly" (sadly a gig I don't even remember); and the fact that "everyone wants to like The Stone Roses at the moment". Not be like them. Just like them. To have some connection with them.

"Vocalist Ian Brown, the unlikeliest hero of the year, has the crowd falling over themselves to get his attention. He skulks around looking mischievous, a wee bit aloof, while the band shimmy through 35 stylish minutes and into the final 'letting loose' instrumental climax.

"They hack down their instruments and amble off leaving the encore shouts to rise and fall, unrequited. They are what favourite bands are all about."

And that was it. They were a group – after a period of uncertainty – that everyone could agree on. A group you didn't want to argue with.

By the end of the year, they were pictured standing at the summit of a mountain with the headline 'Top Of The World'.

Simon got to write the first feature on the Roses for *NME*, but we didn't always land the articles we wanted. I don't think we ever claimed to be the best writers on the paper in 1989 (for a start, we weren't that cocky, and secondly we knew it wasn't true). But that left us in a difficult position. We were going out and finding new bands, and often writing the first introductory pieces on them. But when it came to the follow-up feature or the first cover story (articles that involved trips to Holland or America or, gulp, Japan), then it was the bigger-name scribes who got the job.

So come the end of the year, we didn't get the pay-off junket to New York or Amsterdam. We ended up stranded in Wolverhampton.

It was four weeks till Christmas, and we decided to start the festive celebrations early by reviewing Ned's Atomic Dustbin's big Midlands homecoming show at the Wolverhampton Civic Hall.

Ned's had had a terrific year. They were good fun to watch. And the bill also featured Mega City Four and Senseless Things. So we went and had a marvellous time. The crowd was terrific, and for once, instead of analysing the gig too much, I counted my blessings and sang and smiled and drank copious pints of cider.

After the gig and post-show drinks we staggered into the street, feeling elated, to find it had started snowing. And I don't want to sound too cheesy but life seemed very good.

Life was not so good the following morning when I woke up with an extraordinary hangover and found that the TV in the hotel room wasn't working. Cursing and bumping into things, I made for the bathroom and the light refused to come on. The whole room was broken. Outside in the corridor it wasn't any better. No lights. No lift. No, erm, sound.

I headed down the stairs and into the hotel reception and found myself in a scene from *The Shining*. The place was deserted. There was a single candle burning on the reception desk and there was snow up to the window ledges. I was just waiting for a small boy to creep up muttering 'redrum, redrum…' when a member of staff ran in through one door and out another. Was she being chased by a man with an axe?

No, she was followed by a man in overalls. We were in Wolverhampton in the middle of a blizzard and the whole town had been plunged into chaos by a power cut. But there was worse news to come. After the power was restored, Simon and I checked the travel situation and found that nothing was moving. No buses, definitely no trains all day… and by the way, the town centre is closing at 3.30 p.m. We were stuck. Not only that, but we were stuck in a hotel that we'd only booked for one night – and we were skint.

We sat in the lobby by the Christmas tree and weighed up our options. Then we phoned the Ned's press office to explain our predicament. The girl at the other end of the phone seemed to have some difficulty believing us ("It's not snowing in London," she told us helpfully), but eventually, after convincing her that our only option was to huddle together for warmth in a shop doorway, she said she'd sort something out.

We were due back in London to hand in our review of the Ned's gig in 24 hours' time – and we could barely get out of the hotel, let alone Wolverhampton. And on top of that, all we had for musical inspiration was Sir bleedin' Paul McCartney.

As we sat round the Christmas tree in reception, the hotel's music centre – powered by the emergency generator – jollied into life. And what did it spark up with? 'Simply Having A Wonderful Christmas Time'.

AaaaaarrrggghhhhhhhhhhhhhhhhHHHHHHH.

Alright, it was funny the first time. But it soon became apparent that there were only seven tracks on their Christmas tape. That's one 'Simply Having' every 25 minutes (punctuated by Greg Lake, Jona Lewie, 'Lonely This Christmas' and three other songs I've blocked from memory for fear of going completely doolally).

It was two days before they cleared the tracks and we got a train home.

CHAPTER 8

You Love Us

Whatever you've read is probably wrong. Apart from the date and venue – and aside from the chapter in Simon Price's excellent book *Everything* – the accounts of the night that Manic Street Preachers' guitarist Richey Edwards inscribed the legend '4 REAL' into his arm have been distorted or blown out of all proportion.

For instance, one music paper article, a few years ago, reported that it was me who called the ambulance for Edwards after our ill-fated conversation – while in reality I was standing outside the Norwich Arts Centre, the scene of our showdown, confused, quite shaken up and drawing rather desperately on a cigarette.

If you're unfamiliar with the incident, these are the bare bones of what you need to know. The Manics were an aspiring, ambitious rock'n'roll four-piece from Wales. I was the journalist from the *NME* there in Norwich to review them. After a post-gig interview in which we discussed both their methods and their merits, guitarist Richey Edwards bade me backstage for a final word. Edwards, while still talking, then cut the inscription '4 REAL' into his arm with a razorblade.

Those are the raw facts, the bits of information that I trot out when people stop me at gigs and ask what happened. But those aren't the images that really spring to mind. In order, these are the things I remember most vividly about the '4 REAL' night:

- The cigarette machine at the venue was broken, and photographer Ed Sirrs and I were down to our last Silk Cut.

- Nottingham Forest were playing and bassist Nicky Wire and singer James Dean Bradfield spent their pre-gig downtime in the hotel bar watching the match on TV.

- James was wearing a ludicrously long shiny mac. During the 15-minute drive to the venue, he sat at the back of the bus and refused to be drawn into conversation. I remember thinking: "Well, this is a good start. He hates me and I don't like his coat."

- Richey's eyes.

- The point when the guitarist, in his gorgeous, softly spoken Welsh accent, said: "We are for real." That's the point where we were history.

The Manic Street Preachers had first come to the attention of the *NME* through a self-financed double-A-sided single, 'Suicide Alley'/'Tennessee I Get So Low'. I've still got one somewhere. It has a blue-and-white sleeve featuring a picture of the band on the front striking a pose straight out of The Clash picture book circa 1977.

I'm sure they telephoned and wrote to loads of people around this time (I've got another letter from them, and so had Peelie), but I spoke to the group on the telephone and they were nice people. Eager to progress their career, they said they needed a press officer and asked if I had any ideas. The only person I could suggest of any use was Philip Hall. Hall had been a journalist with the music paper *Record Mirror* before later working for Stiff Records and then starting his own independent PR company, Hall Or Nothing. Philip was a gent. My main dealings with him had been to do with The Sundays and The Stone Roses, who he represented, but his punk/mod background indicated that he might be on a similar wavelength to the Manics.

It transpired that this wasn't a bad call. The Manics approached Hall, who went to see them with his brother Martin in rehearsals in Wales. Despite seeing a band unexpectedly stricken by nerves, they took on the role not just of PR but as their managers as well. In the meantime, another contact-come-friend had arrived on the scene. Ian Ballard from an independent label called Damaged Goods had offered to release the band's next single. Dam Good had started life as a punk and garage reissue label but was branching out into new acts that had the contemporary feel of some of their old-school peers. The Manics were perfect.

Ballard saw the band play at a tiny, but now infamous, gig in a pub near Great Portland Street in London and did a handshake deal with them to record an EP. When it arrived, 'New Art Riot' was an improvement on 'Suicide Alley' but still fell short of what the Manics were reaching for. The same went for some of their gigs. The first time I saw them play was at the Kentish Town Bull and Gate, where they appeared in the same – or similar – boiler-suit chic that had featured on the debut record sleeve.

In a smaller, sweatier club, with the audience slap bang in their face, they would have probably won me over in a shot (this is why I regret not being at the earlier Great Portland Street gig, which had earned them a rave review in *Melody Maker*). But in a deathly quiet, two-thirds empty Bull and Gate they didn't live up to the early press reports. They sounded spindly and looked like they'd come out of a box marked 'punk rock action figures'.

And there was another problem too – and I'll throw my hands up now and admit that it coloured my judgement. I was terrified that we were about to witness a rerun of the rise and fall of Birdland. Some of you might remember them. They were one of the biggest hypes of my time at *NME* (even I ended up being so carried away by their fantastically crazed version of a peroxide blonde Warhol-meets-The Stooges soundclash that I wrote a bloody marvellous front-cover story about them).

Birdland played 30-minute, amphetamine-thrash-pop sets, teased and abused their audience, slated all other 'indie' bands for being dull and unambitious and dressed all in white. With the benefit of hindsight, the Manics were a superior band (they had an appreciation of hip-hop and American rock and art and literature on their side). But at the time a cursory glance at the Manics' manifesto made them look uncomfortably close to what had gone before. Given that Birdland's star had shone and faded within a year, then, in that context, I think a bit of scepticism wasn't uncalled for.

The trouble was, the playful banter began to get out of hand. They released the fantastic 'Motown Junk', their first single for Heavenly and a record I still play regularly at home, at the start of 1991, and we ran with a 'top tips for the year' piece on them. But come the time of the follow-up, 'You Love Us', we'd started to fall out in public. They had a dig at some bands I liked; I had a dig back, making some rather unkind comments about them in a review of another band called Bleach. In retort, they dedicated 'Starlover' to me at their next gig (which I didn't see, but a gleeful Andy Peart phoned me up and told me). It was all a bit petty, but I guess it must have been serious stuff at the time.

Meanwhile, the press they were getting was unswervingly good – and in some cases, from where I was sitting, hilariously sycophantic. When it came to reviewing them on tour, we had a choice. Either we sent someone along who would fawn over them again, or we could go for a more objective opinion. Which is how I ended up going to the Norwich Arts Centre on May 15, 1991.

The first part of the evening, you already know. Ed and myself got a lift to Norwich with Philip, and we booked into a slightly chintzy hotel on the outskirts of town. With the exception of James – then the shyest member of the band – they were, if not chatty, at least amiable enough.

The gig itself was good, but sorely under-attended. In the review it describes the set as "a haze of wanton energy and sketchy punk outbursts. Starting with 'You Love Us' they snap at the heels of an audience split between curiosity and approval – the parochial atmosphere of the gig exaggerated by two people pogoing at the front."

After 33 minutes, the band walked off and the pogoers shouted after them: "Plastic punks!" So, no encore then. Instead, after it had cleared, we sat in the hall and talked about their songs and their vision for the band. Again from the original *NME* piece: "After 30 minutes of friendly enough discussion and vitriol, we wind things up, for the most part agreeing to disagree. It was a good, if clichéd confrontation (maybe leaving both sides a little unsettled)."

The transcript of the interview has been printed elsewhere, and yes, there are questions I asked which seem oddly irrelevant now – but there were some pertinent points too. It certainly wasn't as confrontational as some people have reported. There was also no forewarning of what would happen next. Believe me, backstage, as Richey began to carve his arm open, I was as shocked as anybody was.

People always ask me, why didn't you stop him? And there were two reasons, I think. One is that it happened so quickly. The cuts were deliberate but fast (and got faster and lighter as he neared the end). The second is: do you think he wanted me to stop him?

I don't know exactly how long we talked for after the deed was done, but it was probably about three or four minutes. It was difficult to snap out of. Apart from the odd moment where Richey had looked down to inspect his work, we'd been staring fixedly at each other throughout. But then the conversation was going around in circles – and Richey's arm was beginning to look uncomfortably gory. The blood from the first cut had started to trickle down his arm the moment he'd finished it. (Fact: until I saw the photos the next day, I didn't know what he'd written because it was obscured by the blood.)

"We better do something about that… you're going to mess up their carpet."

Richey looked down at his arm, and then up again, and agreed. At least he gave a faint nod. And that was it. While he stayed put, I went to search for Philip, finding him back in the main hall in conversation with a guy I didn't know. Trying not to set alarm bells ringing, I tugged at Hall's arm and muttered conspiratorially: "I think you should go and see Richey. He's a bit shaken up."

Hall, a quizzical expression crossing his face, excused himself and sauntered backstage. Two minutes later he re-emerged at double-speed and darted off to find a phone or locate the nearest hospital. I found Ed, commandeered our final cigarette and stood outside the venue till it was time to leave.

No one spoke much on the journey back to London. We listened to a compilation tape I'd made up, and then I dozed off in the back seat. Philip dropped us off in the middle of Soho, near one of those 24-hour picture-processing studios that Ed used to use to develop his photos overnight, while I trawled the mini-cab offices trying to find a car back to Brixton. When I got in, my girlfriend awoke briefly and asked how it went.

"Oh, the gig wasn't bad. Not many people there. Then we did the interview and Richey cut his arm open with a razorblade."

"Oh. Right," she said. Then fell asleep again.

It wasn't until the following morning that the incident started to sink in. Apart from the girlfriend ("Was I dreaming, or when you got in, did you say he slashed his arm open?"), the rest of the day was spent explaining what had happened: first to *NME* editor Danny Kelly – the only man in the office when I arrived – and then to the rest of the staff as they filtered into work. Ed arrived with the photos around noon and the debate over whether we should print them or not started in earnest. To add to the unusually dramatic scenes in the office, social commentator and comedian Mark Thomas was on hand – making a documentary about a week in the life of the *NME*. After two relatively tedious days, he finally had a scoop (you can hear part of the programme on the CD version of the Manics' 'Suicide Is Painless').

My favourite quote came from Ed, who through the hubbub can be heard saying, "It's a mint wound." If you know Ed, then that's so him. But the arguments raged on round the lightbox, as people took it in turns with the magnifying viewer to examine the slides. I went back to the live desk and opened some post.

There were two telephone calls that day that put the incident into perspective. The first was from a press officer, who hinted that Richey had privately done this sort of thing before; that he had a history of self-mutilation. And the second was from Richey himself. By a twist of fate, I wasn't there when he called. I was in our regular haunt, the Stamford Arms, explaining what had happened to a couple of my live desk team. (I think, without wanting to sound too melodramatic, I may have been in a state of delayed shock. Sam Steele, then an *NME* freelance but later a Radio 1 producer, claims I was white as a sheet.) I subsequently lost the answerphone tape with his message on it but the gist was "I'm sorry if I upset you in any way, but I was just trying to make my point".

The *NME* ran with a news piece on page three – certainly the goriest page three picture of all time – and my review of the gig led the live section. Of everything I wrote while I was at the paper, this was one of the most difficult pieces to construct. But some of it still stands up. This is from the conclusion: "There's no doubt that they are a thorn in the side of rock at the moment. That goes without saying. And agreed, what wouldn't we give for a new political pop band back in the charts? Someone who'd go further than just being worthy. But the fact is I'm not sure the Manics have everything under control at the moment."

The backlash was amazing. The Manics for their part took the incident and the pictures and used them in evidence against me (but, fair play, I probably might have done the same thing if I were them). The famous 'mint wound' photo was also used later on posters as part of their campaign to break America.

Meanwhile, I stopped going out for a couple of days, because the incessant demands for graphic reruns of the story began to pall. The most stark reaction didn't happen until a couple of years later, though. Journalist Andrew Smith travelled to Thailand with the band for a feature in *The Face* magazine. At the end of a gig he spoke with some of their fans, and reprinted snippets of the conversation in the final article.

"We understand why Richey did what he did," said one Manic supporter. "We have a culture of self-mutilation in this country. And if Steve Lamacq ever comes here, we will... KILL HIM."

To make matters worse, I was reading the piece on a Tube train, and found myself immediately looking around for possible signs of an assassination attempt.

It's not the only feedback I've had from Manics fans down the years. Every year on the anniversary of Richey's disappearance I get a letter saying: "I don't know how you sleep at night having driven him to do what he did." And I'd like to write back with my version of events, and how I don't believe I drove him to anything, but it strikes me that people like this have made up their minds that I am the devil – and always will be. And that's fine.

We only saw each other once more before he vanished. Richey and James were reviewing the singles for *NME* and I stood in the lift with them, along with Philip and, I think, Simon Williams. There was total silence as they stared at their shoes right up to the twenty-fifth floor.

But to all intents and purposes the Manics feud ended on the tragic note of Philip's death from cancer. It was an event that hit Richey hardest, but we were all affected in our own ways. I didn't know Philip even half as well as they did – after all, the Manics had even lived with Hall and his wife Terri for a while – but he was one of the few real good guys I knew and probably the first close death I'd experienced while in the industry.

I phoned Hall Or Nothing to check if it would be OK to play a Manics track dedicated to Philip on that night's *Evening Session*. A hour or so later I got a call back from Nicky Wire and we went ahead with a short tribute on the programme.

Since then, I've spoken to them on many occasions. The first of them was when James came on the *Session* shortly after Richey's disappearance, followed in 1998 with a programme we made for Radio 1 about the success of *Everything Must Go*, after which we went to the pub and talked music and football and got on really well. And, of course, they've been on the 6 Music show numerous times since then.

And I'm not sure if it's because we're not angry young men any more, or whether we've found different targets for our ire, but in a strange way it feels like we're all on the same side now. Maybe our ageing insecurities are falling into sync.

POSTSCRIPT: In spring 2018, when the Manics appeared on our show, discussing their new album *Resistance Is Futile* and then reviewing the week's new releases on *Roundtable*, there was an earth-shattering moment off air, when, for the first time *in nearly 30 years*, Nicky Wire and I agreed on a band we both liked. Step forward Idles, your place in pop music history is assured.

CHAPTER 9

A Song From Under The Floorboards

The now defunct pop bible *Smash Hits* saved my life scores of times when I was a kid. This is what would happen. I'd have had a song stuck in my head for days – but you know what it's like, the singer mumbles at one point and you can't quite make out what he's saying, and after a while you think you're going to go mad unless you know what it is. So I'd go to the newsagent and feverishly look up the words in *Smash Hits*. I think even then I wanted to know not only what the words were, but what they *meant*.

But that wasn't the end of it. How many times have you looked up a set of lyrics only to find that the band hasn't been singing what you thought they were singing. Not only that, but their version is somehow inferior (the one in your head, the one you've wanted to believe, is ten times better than the real thing).

Smash Hits was a cruel mistress – as are the hundreds of lyric websites out there now. Lyrics – forcibly separated from the bosom of the music – can look terrifically lost and lonely. There's nowhere to hide. There's a serious point here somewhere, but first: the funniest thing I ever saw in *Smash Hits* (that's if you exclude the words to 'Tattva' by Kula Shaker). During the late seventies, there was a stream of chart hits – which I like to remember as wally disco. It was a DJ who came up with the name. Wally disco encompassed all the records that sounded like they'd been recorded specifically for wedding receptions and your sister's eighteenth birthday party.

The epidemic of wally disco records left *Smash Hits* with a problem. Wally disco worked solely on the basis that the more words you used, the harder it would be for people to sing along. Forget the mercurial minimalists of the American lo-fi scene – this is where pop music's grasp of the theory 'less is more' truly succeeded.

At the top of the wally disco heap was a track called 'Dance Yourself Dizzy' by Liquid Gold. *Smash Hits* must have pissed themselves as they were laying it out – but all credit to them, as they printed the words in full. The opening line was:

> "D-d-d-d-d-d-d-d-d-d-d-d-d-d-d-d-d-d-d-d-d-d-d-d-d-d-d-d-d-dizzzy."

These days I still like to know what lyrics say, but I'm less keen on finding out what they mean to the person who wrote them. I remember interviewing Blur at the time of *Modern Life Is Rubbish* and saying how great the track 'Chemical World' was because of the line 'they sleep together so they don't get lonely', which struck me as a harsh but sometimes true image of London life. People get bored or lost and they end up in bed with someone because it alleviates the tedium. Or it stops them having to find a real solution to why they were bored or lost in the first place.

But, of course, that's not what the song meant in Damon's head. It wasn't even the right words (Damon says 'stick together' instead of 'sleep together' and so the song means something else entirely). But after he told me, the song never sounded as good again.

And I've done this with scores of other bands (though not recently). I'll have a beautifully concocted picture of what the lyrics are driving at – and Jack White or Alex Turner or whoever will look across the 6 Music desk and do one of two things. Either they smile sympathetically, or they just launch into the real reason why they wrote the track. But that's not what we want to hear. We just want them to agree with us.

It goes back to the way we personalise pop music to suit our own needs. I obviously came up with my crappy sociology lecture

Issue three of my fanzine *A Pack Of Lies* with a frankly inexplicable cover. It did have quite a good article about Brookside in it though.

The cover of the final issue of *A Pack Of Lies*, which featured a collage of rejection letters sent to Uxbridge band The Price, whose guitarist Leigh Heggarty was an occasional contributor (and these days plays in Ruts DC).

When not blagging free drinks on tour, Teenage Fan Club enjoyed nothing more than weightlifting with *NME* journalists. An out-take from the photoshoot for their first *NME* cover story.

Manic post stage-dive grin in the crowd at the front for Carter (USM)'s gig in Paris.

Lurking in the background of Martyn Goodacre's Nirvana photoshoot in Shepherds Bush in the autumn of 1990. I have no explanation for that denim jacket.
MARTYN GOODACRE

PAUL COX 081 800 4490/081 969 1289
RICHARD ROBERTS 081 800 4490/0992 711828
MANAGEMENT FOR TH' FAITH HEALERS, CRANE & HEADCLEANER

Steve,

I'm sending this P.J. Harvey tape because think it is one of the more interesting demos we've d sent us this year and I'd be dead keen on ur opinion on it. They are a three-piece from Yeovil orset fronted by Polly Harvey (hence the name) who ha t done a few gigs with friends the Becketts.

Hopefully they'll be in town to play with Sun rriage and Midway Still at the White Horse on 27 ly and then again on August 31st at the Falcon th the Sunflowers.

With thanks Paul Cox

he letter that accompanied the first PJ Harvey demo, sent to me at the *NME* by Paul Cox, one half of the duo who aunched the excellent Too Pure label. Polly subsequently came to London for her first *NME* interview, conducted in a orner of The Stamford Arms pub.

Manic Street Preachers
15 St Tudors View,
Blackwood,
Gwent NP2 1AQ.
Tel: 0495 222123

Dear Steve,

Heres our new demo & information ect...... I hope it conveys a sense of purpose to eradicate the desire to trip out and tune in (89) & instead fuck up & ignore "channel apathy drug". We just want to play anytime and anywhere as we just want to play live NOW! We have no regard for our bodies, ... We just want to waste away under speed excess and bleed to death on our own bar chord overdose. We might record this demo as a single and release it on ~~perhaps~~ Damaged Goods, soon, so could you consider including us in 'Rave on' or your 'turn ons'

I love, M.S. Preachers X

P.S. If we do some London dates could you come?.

The Manic Street Preachers missive that arrived with a demo featuring the tracks that did indeed end up on the Damaged Goods label as the 'New Art Riot' EP. The homemade demo sleeve had a picture of me, cut from the paper, with an arrow pointing at it and the words "cheek bone charisma" scribbled by the side.

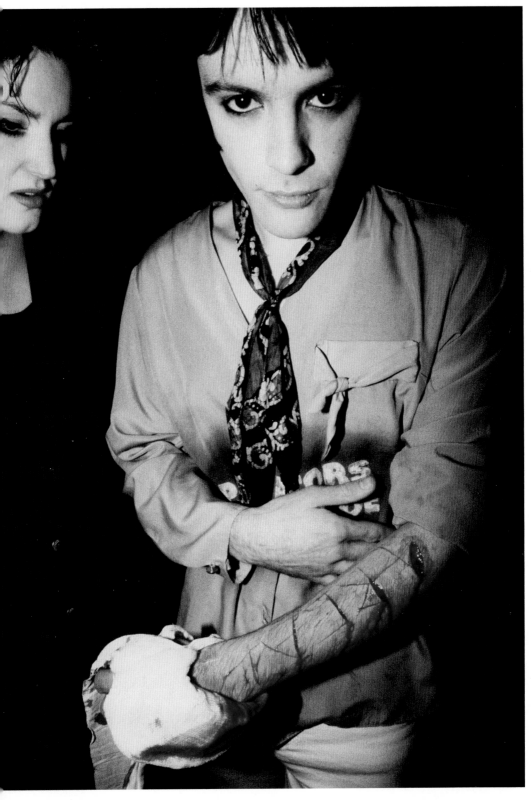

Richey Edwards post interview, following their gig at Norwich Arts Centre: the now famous Ed Sirrs photo of the 'mint wound'.

The
Music
Method

One Christopher Place Chalton Street London NW1 1JF 01 388 7826

5th December 1989

Steve Lamacq
NME
Kings Reach Tower
Stamford Street
SE1 9LS

Dear Steve,

I spoke to you the other day about **SEYMOUR** and hope that they prove to be what everyone has been telling you!

I enclose a tape with two tracks as well as a list of forthcoming gigs.

Hope you enjoy the tape and see you at the Cricketers.

Best wishes

Marijke Bergkamp

The covering note that came with Seymour's two track demo at the end of 1989, recorded at The Beat Factory featuring versions of 'She's So High' and 'Fool'.

NME staff and freelancers celebrate at a party in 1990 to mark a rise in circulation that took sales back up past the 100,000 mark. Among them Danny Kelly (left, glasses), legendary rock photographer Kevin Cummins (flailing in his hand in front of me) next to Stuart Maconie and future *Loaded* magazine editor James Brown. Front centre, Editor Alan Lewis, without whom, none of this would have been possible.
TIM JARVIS

Up The U's! Note our club sponsors at one point in the mid-nineties were SGR, the local Colchester commercial radio station!

explanation of the Blur song because that's what I wanted it to mean. Either that or I'd got out of bed on the wrong side and wanted the world to be an awful place – and this made it sound as awful as possible.

I can twist hundreds of songs round to fit me. I like feeling part of a song because I like knowing that someone else feels the same way I do. Or at least I think they feel the same. It makes me feel like one of the chosen few. That all makes some sort of sense to me.

So why, once we've found a record that is indisputably about ourselves, do we go round quoting it to other people? Is it a cry for help?

"Look, don't you see what this song says about me?"

I've done it myself. I've resorted to quoting lyrics at people in the hope that I will sound more enigmatic – and that my life will appear stranger or more complex or interesting. But deep down I never hold out much hope that it'll work.

So I've tried to resist the temptation to quote lyrics in this book, but sod it. In this case, I'm going to allow myself to make an exception. I don't own that many books about music, but I have one called *It Only Looks As If It Hurts*, the complete lyrics of Howard Devoto from 1976 to 1990. Devoto was originally in the Buzzcocks but left to form Magazine, and then when Magazine split he formed Luxuria.

It's the Magazine days that interest me the most. That's when Devoto wrote 'A Song From Under The Floorboards'. And that's me. In those lines. All over the place.

> I am angry, I am ill and I'm as ugly as sin
> My irritability keeps me alive and kicking
> I know the meaning of life, it doesn't help me a bit
> I know beauty and I know a good thing when I see it
>
> This is a song from under the floorboards
> This is a song from where the wall is cracked
> My force of habit, I am an insect
> I have to confess I'm proud as hell of that fact
>
> I know the highest and the best
> I accord them all due respect

But the brightest jewel inside of me
Glows with pleasure at my own stupidity

This is a song from under the floorboards...

I'll probably have to find their live album *Play* now and stick the track on and sing along to it. And there's another danger in investing in lyrics. The singing along thing. It's something else I've suffered from. It's not so bad at home where people can't hear or see you. It's not even too bad, I suppose, if you're at a gig and there are loads of other people joining in. But in the past I've found myself singing along to songs by obscure indie bands in the back rooms of pubs. Or worse, mouthing the words. I've caught myself doing it (or seen other people watching me aghast) but it's just an instinctive reaction. It just, as Devoto might say, 'pours out of me'.

CHAPTER 10

After The Watershed

It's been very slow going, these last two days. I've gone back in time and I've got stuck. If anyone calls, you'll have to tell them I'm in 1990.

There are music papers all over the floor and old 12-inch singles by the stereo – and I think I'm suffering from thousand-yard stare. (In fact, there was a band called Thousand Yard Stare who I went to the Shetland Islands with in 1991. We came home by ferry and I was violently ill for three hours. They recently reformed and we recount the story of this trip like it was The Beatles at Chez Stadium mixed with *The Wicker Man*.) I'm an indie-war vet, reliving the conflict of the start of the nineties.

If 1989 had been some sort of dress rehearsal for the new decade, 1990 and 1991 were the real thing. I don't think any of us particularly thought at the time that we were involved with setting the agenda for the next few years. But in retrospect, much of what happened – and many of the bands who emerged during that time – did end up shaping the nineties. There was Blur, the Manics, The Charlatans and *Nevermind* by Nirvana. There was the first Prodigy single, Radiohead and P. J. Harvey, who I was lucky enough to interview for her first *NME* feature: a 400-word rave review based on an hour we shared in the Stamford Arms, a shady boozer found five minutes from our offices.

There was so much going on that it was hard to know where to start. The way the *NME* started each week was with an editorial meeting every Tuesday at around 12 o'clock. A wrapped bundle of the new issue – out on Tuesday in London, but Wednesday around the rest of the country – would arrive in the reception and everyone would hurry over to get a copy. The editorial meeting followed. It was partly a debrief, raking over the highs and lows of the previous week's issue (including endless complaints from writers over who'd had their copy cut). But mostly editorials were about the following week's edition. Who was going to be on the cover? Who's the lead live review? Who the hell can we get to do the Pet Shop Boys again?

When people ask how the paper worked, I'd try to explain it like this. Imagine if you took a bunch of musicians who all liked different styles of music, put them in a studio together, and told them to make a record. That's what our editorial meetings were like. A lot of people banging different drums. Very loudly.

During the *NME*'s celebrations for its fortieth anniversary, former writer turned TV and radio personality Danny Baker was asked to comment on his stint at the paper in the seventies. I can't remember the quote word for word, but the gist was: "Everybody thinks their time at the *NME* is the best. We all think it goes downhill after we leave."

Danny – you are spot on. So I am honour-bound to claim that the team at the *NME* at the start of the nineties was one of the all-time greats. OK, we disagreed at length – at least once every week – and me and the LP editor Stuart Bailie tried unwisely to launch a ska revival at one point, but we were pretty good. Alan Lewis had moved on to become publisher, so Danny Kelly took over as editor with the whizz-kid James Brown on features. When Brown took off to pursue other projects, Andrew Collins replaced him. And the paper had two deputy editors: Brendon Fitzgerald, the indomitable leader of the subs room, and Stuart Maconie.

Together, it was a precariously balanced but determined team. So when the paper was good, it was genuinely good, and when it was bad – when you saw another two-bit band being handed a feature on the basis of one crap single, or you saw press office hype triumphing over common sense – well, then, then… Oh it made you want to scream.

It's something that came up in conversation when writing this book, discussing my stint at *NME* with someone who knew me very well at the time.

"I was angry all the time in 1991, wasn't I?" (Obviously hoping the answer was no.)

"Yes."

"All the time?"

"ALL THE TIME," they laughed. It's funny. It wasn't so much anger, but journalistic indignation and petulance. We all have it at times. Because we are right and the rest of the world is wrong. And if push comes to shove, then MY BAND IS ALWAYS BETTER THAN YOUR BAND!

"You're not so bad now," they added. "You don't get like that *so often*."

But I still do it. Even now, I still throw the toys out of the pram. I still get upset with the machinations of the industry and the perceived injustice when a band you like doesn't get the breaks. In short, life still isn't fair.

And I think that's why the start of the nineties is a difficult time to reassess for me. Reading some of the reviews I wrote then, I can see a cheeky, sarcastic, angry side of myself that I thought I might grow out of. But, I have to admit, it's still there lurking in the background. I can still have a good row about pop music and therefore it must still mean enough to me to carry on.

It's a twisted logic, I suppose, but it'll have to do for now.

But back at the start of the nineties, Simon Williams and I were on some kind of indie underground crusade, if that's not too pompous a claim. The upshot of this was a ruthless and often unkind dismissal of anyone signed to a big label who we didn't rate. And a steadfast loyalty to any band who wore threadbare T-shirts, looked like they last saw the inside of a barbers 18 months ago and were 'signed' to a label run out of a bedroom in an unfashionable corner of East London or a backstreet in Leeds.

As an example, here are the highs and lows from a singles page in August 1991. By the way, baggy Liverpool band The Farm were on the cover. And the big album review was of the debut record by Paris Angels (who someone gave nine out of ten to).

So, my Single Of The Week One: Midway Still with 'I Won't Try'. Single Of The Week Two: 'Charly' by The Prodigy (and I quote: "a good, busy, bassy club record"). I'd heard the Prodigy track on Radio 1's *Big Beat* show while driving to a gig in Harlow. It's one of the few occasions when I've pulled off the road and stopped to hear who it was by. But anyway… if those records represented my twin visions of what pop should stand for that week, then the next one was the Antichrist.

The Blessing: 'Flames' (MCA Records). "The very fact that The Blessing record exists means that someone at MCA genuinely believes that they will sell lots of records. If this person would like to get in touch I'll cheerfully bet them a tenner that they won't."

You might think that was a bit harsh, but there was worse to come. Not only did we not much care for the bland syrup being doled out by the major labels, we didn't much like daytime Radio 1 either. This review got me a new catchphrase that other staffers used to quote at me. And yes, I am aware of the definition of irony.

The Origin: 'Set Sails Free' (Hut). "The press release of The Origin record makes a point of saying that their last single was played 35 times by Radio 1… just the sort of simpering thing you expect to find attached to Bands-Desperately-Trying-To-Crack-It who haven't got a following, or worse, any sense of passion. As if being played 35 times by Radio 1 is some justification for existing, or benchmark of talent. YOU TOOLS!"

In my defence, I wasn't the only one who was ranting and screaming my way through life. After leaving the news desk I became the paper's live reviews editor and set about building a team of freelancers around me who were equally obsessed, deranged and enthusiastic. That makes perfect sense to me. What makes less sense is that for a while I tried to persuade them that they all had to call me 'Guv'. Don't ask (too many repeats of *The Sweeney*?).

Several good writers were already there (Williams, Dele Fadele, Gina Morris). To add to them, when one of the rival papers, *Sounds*, was shut down, I managed to persuade Keith Cameron – one of their best and most informed writers – to join *NME*. He was joined by future *Select* magazine editor and broadsheet political scribe John Harris, who I wheedled away from *Melody Maker*, and a very tall man called Johnny Cigarettes. Cigs was one of the few writers we found from the pile of unsolicited reviews that used to clog up one end of the live desk.

Every music paper used to be sent unsolicited material from would-be writers, but like bands and demos, the quality was usually quite suspect. The competition for work was incredibly fierce and you needed to stand out from the crowd to get a look-in. Cigs – all six foot of him – stood out like a sore thumb. His writing was funny and acerbic and he used to take the piss out of anything that moved. I tried phoning the number he'd enclosed with the two trial reviews he'd sent, but got no reply for days.

Little did we know that he worked the graveyard shift at a petrol station near Leamington Spa, so he'd go to gigs by night, write the reviews between serving people packets of Rizlas and Lucozade, and then sleep through the day. How can you not employ someone like that? So Cigs started freelancing, as did a girl called Sam Steele who got her break by telling me that the paper's dance coverage was crap. After an hour of being verbally beaten up I gave in. "OK then. I'll give you a trial run next week," I told her. "Sorry, I'm going to Goa for a month," she replied. "I'll phone you when I get back."

The live desk war office moved from the Stamford Arms to the Doggett's Coat and Badge (partly because it had a better pinball table). In the days before computer discs, the freelancers used to deliver their typed hard copy to the pub. Then Simon and I would go through the live diary – our scrawled list of gigs that needed covering – and we'd divvy up work for the following week. I've never known a lifestyle like it. We worked incredibly hard and we hit our deadlines, but at the same time we'd be gigging most nights and falling into the pub at lunch. Either we'd discuss bands or we'd get into arguments about the direction of the paper.

It's not surprising that the war office occasionally lost the plot. Starved of sleep and wound up by the editorial policy – which, of course, was too safe in our view – we'd sometimes let the ranting get out of hand. So in the week that the features staff decided that we should have The Beautiful South on the cover (AGAIN!), I took it into my own hands to discuss this affront with Danny Kelly. Fuelled by three lunchtime pints of Addlestones cider, I strode back to our building and marched into his office.

The big new band at the time, just cracking the Top 40, was an Irish trio called The Frank and Walters. Let's put them on the front instead, I whined. Danny, quite sanely, explained the popularity of the South and the level of interest in them. At which point we traded verbal blows for a couple of minutes before I shouted something unrepeatable and stormed back out, slamming the door behind me.

Forgetting that I was a grown-up 20-something man and not a stroppy small boy, I kicked the nearest piece of office furniture (a chair, which turned out to be made of concrete). I managed to get as far as the coffee machine in the corridor outside the office before having to sit down and take one of my DMs off. By the time I went to put it back on, the swelling was so large that the boot didn't fit any more. I ended up in casualty at St Thomas's Hospital.

"So, Mr Lamacq, how did you do this?"

"I kicked a chair," I mumbled. Quite rightly, they sent me to the back of the queue and I waited three hours for an X-ray and a pair of crutches. Back home the next day, the *NME* sent round a home-made 'Get Well Soon' card. It had my head superimposed on the body of a prostrate man with a broken leg in plaster. In massive 72-point letters at the top, it simply said: 'You Tool'.

By the spring of 1990 I'd done all kinds of daft things, but I hadn't stagedived. Stagediving was big in the early nineties. Virtually every gig we went to featured people clambering up on stage and then launching themselves at the heads of the third row.

And I don't know why, but it never really appealed that much – except maybe out of curiosity. So my sole attempt came at the end of a long and difficult day on the road with Carter (USM). I'd been sent with photographer Ed Sirrs to review the band live in Paris. But that wasn't all. *NME* had discovered that Carter had given an 'exclusive' interview to *Melody Maker*, which was due to run as a cover story in the following issue. Our job was to try to sneak our own interview with them and then run a spoiler story with a live photo on the front of the *NME* the same week.

I wasn't entirely comfortable with this. It's a journalistic trick which used to happen quite often, but I'd never stitched up a group before – especially a band I knew. Consequently, I decided to get as drunk as possible to give me some courage. This wasn't difficult. As an experiment, Carter's label Chrysalis had decided to send us out to France via City Airport – the business-oriented airport in the East End of London. Ed in his shades and me in my Mega City Four fleece must have set the drug-runner alarms alight as every security man we passed gave us the evils and we were questioned at length as they checked our bags.

Once on the plane, however, we found we'd been assigned to the business class section, which meant you were entitled to as much free champagne as you could possibly handle at 11.30 in the morning. We arrived in Paris and checked in at the hotel. Then we went straight on to the venue, where, having made up a story about needing some quotes to flesh out the review, I got an interview and felt thoroughly rotten about it the entire way through.

It wasn't just Carter I knew. It was some of their crew as well. At one point before the gig I happened to tell the guitar tech that I was thinking of breaking my stagediving duck, and that I'd picked France because no one would see me if I fell through the crowd and landed flat on my face. (There had been a story doing the rounds of a *Maker* writer who had leapt off stage expecting to land in the grateful arms of the adoring audience. But the crowd had parted and he'd fallen straight to the floor.)

Halfway through the gig, I managed to position myself on the side of the stage, kneeling just behind singer Jim Bob's amp. As I got up to look at the crowd and to try to pick the softest people to land on, the guitar tech thought he would help out and gave me a firm push. All of a sudden I was on the stage, vaguely aware I was heading past Jim Bob and towards the crowd.

There is a picture of me in the sweaty throng, taken just after I'd come down to earth. The smile is not one of ecstasy. It's one of pure relief.

We put Carter on the cover with one of Ed's live shots. I dug out the issue the other day and it looks quite good. A few pages after the Carter piece was the only bit of writing I'd contributed to the paper that week – a review of *Nevermind* by Nirvana.

CHAPTER 11

Freak Scene

I can't remember exactly when it was, but sometime in the early eighties I received a home-made compilation tape through the post from a fanzine in America. I can't even remember the name of the fanzine, but I remember the impact that the cassette had. I sat in my bedroom in a curious daze. It was like being back in double maths trying to learn how to multiply fractions.

What on earth was all this stuff? Who were TSOL? How great were these bands Social Distortion and Descendents? How FAST were Hüsker Dü? What am I going to send the fanzine back in return?

The American bands seemed immediately more eloquent than the second generation of punk-inspired groups in Britain. They were more incisive and cutting, and in Hüsker Dü's case, extreme.

I'd heard Dead Kennedys, who were the most notorious US punk group of the time, and I was aware of Black Flag. But I hadn't taken much notice of them, because, naively, I didn't believe the Americans really knew what they were doing. I thought they were cheating at school, trying to copy what was now a British-owned rebellion. Then the tape arrived, and with it came my introduction to hardcore – which would eventually lead me and many others to Nirvana.

The more I read up on the history of punk, the more it seemed like there was a huge game of transatlantic tennis going on with guitar music as the ball. In very simplistic terms, could we say that the Americans invented punk and then didn't know what to do with it? So they served to us. In a return cross-court volley, we gave them back the Sex Pistols. Upping the ante, they struck back with Dead Kennedys, and then, bless us, we hit them with GBH and The Exploited. And possibly coined the term 'thrash-punk'.

Obviously, this is a bit of a cack-handed theory, but the evolution of punk and then hardcore music has often seen Britain and America taking a sound or a scene and then refining it into a new image.

Back at the *A Pack Of Lies* HQ, I thrilled to '1945' by Social Distortion, but it was The Descendents who really blew me off the edge of my bed. There were two tracks by them on the tape – I later found both of them on the album *Milo Goes To College* (because Milo, the singer, was, erm, off to college). They sounded unproduced and edgy and had these wonderful hook lines. And the bass sound was so different to British records. It was more taut and tense. It was the same bass sound that later turned up on the first Fugazi album, which was another mind-blowing record.

In the meantime, the hardcore scene continued to evolve in America, watched closely by bands and fans in this country. The labels of choice at the time for many of us were Dischord and SST Records. SST had Descendents, who, after Milo's departure, recruited a new singer and re-emerged as All, and Dischord had Minor Threat. Minor Threat were straight-edge (this, I think, was a new concept to Britain), which meant they didn't drink or smoke. And they looked hard as nails. Have you noticed how the British guitar groups of the eighties looked so flimsy and underfed that they might just blow away, while the Americans came with tattoos and muscles and skinheads? Or am I just thinking of Henry Rollins?

There was a definite underground community growing around these groups – boosted, I guess, around this time by the skateboard kids and the first signs of American punk fashion. How much does it say about our differing approaches to pop clobber that the Americans gave punk fleeces and shorts – and we gave it the bum flap?

It had all the criteria for being a cult scene in the eighties. It received very little press and never troubled the charts, but when the bands played in the UK they sold out wherever they went. With the exception of maybe the ever-improving Hüsker Dü, the ultra-lazy Dinosaur Jr. and the incredibly hip Sonic Youth (who have their own special place in this story), it was a music that survived in a world of fanzines and transit vans. That would all change, though, from the end of the eighties onwards.

At the *NME* it was clear that something was happening in Seattle, even if we couldn't quite focus on what it was. Our pre-grunge specialist was Edwin Pouncey – aka cartoonist Savage Pencil – who regularly filed reports on bands emerging on American labels like Sub Pop and the even harder to find Sympathy For The Record Industry (who would later release an ace seven-inch by a group called Hole).

But the question was: where did the bands with ludicrous names and incredible hair fit in? It was 1989, the year of Madchester, and here we were being invaded by these nightmare visions of proto-grunge chic. It was quite exciting, to be honest. As more and more British bands started namechecking cult US groups – and the gig circuit began to expand and grow again after a period in the doldrums – the American groups started turning up on a regular basis. Mudhoney, for instance, seemed to be on tour every week, either with or without heavyweight labelmates Tad.

Both *Melody Maker* and *Sounds* leapt on the Seattle scene, and finally at *NME* we followed suit. In the end-of-year issue for 1989, Pouncey – already up to his waist in filthy guitar slurry – wrote favourably about Soundgarden (already signed to A&M after spells at Sub Pop and SST), Mudhoney and Mother Love Bone. "But there are other huge talents to be found on Sub Pop," he added. "Nirvana are one with Kurdt Kobain proving himself to be a master songwriter."

The description 'master songwriter' I find interesting now (more so than the different spelling of Kurdt's name). Everything written about Sub Pop and the new harsher, hairier American bands of the time enthused about the noise and the frenzied sound of the Seattle groups. But songwriting? That was a new one.

For my part, Nirvana's debut album *Bleach* virtually passed me by. I had a copy. Quite liked it. Moved on. What rescued me from being a Nirvana nobody was a tape that arrived from their press officer, Anton Brookes. Anton, a gentle giant of PR, knew more than most about the American hardcore scene having worked out of an office at Southern Distribution (who handled vast quantities of the stuff), and represented groups like Fugazi and Mudhoney.

The tape itself, badly copied onto a TDK C60, featured Nirvana's next single, 'Sliver', and some demos of tracks that would later go to make up their second album. 'Sliver' was just pop genius. If you listen back to it, it's a phenomenally to-the-point record. There's the loping bass, Kurt's vocals and then a sudden surge of guitar which induces Kurt's screaming chorus line. Other grunge records were noisier, but Nirvana's were more structured and expressive.

The single's release was delayed for weeks. Can't remember why, but I have the press release that came with it. It describes 'Sliver' as the greatest Nirvana experience, "catching the power trio in its transitional, creatively enhanced state". Not a bad summarisation, really. The final paragraph is more oblique: "When will there be a Nirvana LP? Nobody knows. Who's drumming? It's that guy from Scream, and Kurdt says he's great… New stuff? We'll let you know."

The confusion surrounding their future was understandable. Yes, after employing Dan Peters from Mudhoney to drum on 'Sliver', they'd recruited a new drummer, Dave Grohl. And having outgrown Sub Pop/Tupelo Recordings they were in negotiation with various new labels. As they arrived for a mini-tour of the UK at the end of 1990, Island Records were very keen, I remember, but the band still seemed non-committal. We got our interview the night after the band had played in Norwich and had returned to the bed and breakfast hotel in Shepherd's Bush where they were staying. Kurt looked tired, bassist Krist Novoselic had "one of your British colds", and drummer Grohl was rooting through a bin liner full of dirty laundry accumulated over the past few days of touring.

NME freelance photographer Martyn Goodacre took the pictures. It was freezing cold, but he managed to cajole the group outside and set about photographing them at a bus stop, in a laundrette, and on a playground climbing frame (at one point Cobain hung upside down from the frame, his legs wrapped over the top bars). Right at the very end of the session, with the band's enthusiasm draining away, Martyn got *the* shot – the one that was eventually used as a cover picture when Cobain killed himself in 1994. It's the one with the huge eyes, staring out from beneath his fringe.

Some of these pictures can be found in the excellent Nirvana book *Winterland* – a pictorial record of the group throughout their career. Of the rest of the set, there's a particularly bizarre one of the band walking across a zebra crossing, with Novoselic puffing his chest out and impersonating a monkey. Over the other side of the road, with crap hair and an ill-fitting denim jacket, you can just about see me laughing.

There was no disguising the fact that they were knackered. We did the interview in their two-room HQ in the B&B, Novoselic retiring fully clothed to his bed and hiding under the duvet for the entire interview, only poking his head out when he had something to contribute. Kurt sat next to me on another bed, staring at the floor. Grohl got on with washing his socks in the bathroom. In the corner of the room, one of those small, wall-hung TVs was showing *The Wizard of Oz*. It was all very strange.

Before talking about music, Kurt revealed that he kept turtles as pets at home in his bath. "They have no personality at all," he said. "And I like that in a pet."

But the most important revelations were about their music. Having spent the *Bleach* era concerned that their melodic side might alienate them from a punk audience, Nirvana were starting to loosen up. There was positive talk of the recent Sonic Youth album *Goo* – the Youth's most accessible record to date – and they didn't flinch when I said they could end up following the REM route out of the leftfield and into the charts.

"We're finally coming out of the drains and saying we like pop music," Cobain added. "So if we want to write a song like REM we'll do that, or if I want to write a song like Godflesh I'll do that."

In the next few months, the Nirvana bandwagon slowly began to roll. They signed with Geffen and went off to record *Nevermind*. And when the tapes of the album finally turned up, you could tell they'd cracked it. I'd love to be able to tell you that I foresaw the worldwide mayhem that was to follow within the next 18 months. But I didn't. We knew, those of us in the office who were already converts, that this was a massively important record; that the sound of it would be influential in the future; and that Nirvana had now surpassed anything previously achieved in the grunge genre. But the commercial success that slowly gathered momentum over the following year was a surprise even to us. Back in the States I suspect it was a shock to some of the Geffen staff too, who hadn't exactly gone overboard at the start with their recording and video budgets for the band.

But all this partly explains why, when the *NME* came to review it, the album was relegated to the fourth page of the paper's album section.

Mind you, it hadn't struck lucky with the competition it was up against. The other major albums reviewed in that week's issue were: *Screamadelica*, the future Mercury Music Prize-winning and highly influential album from Primal Scream; The Pixies' *Trompe Le Monde* (ironically a band Kurt had a lot of time for); and *Use Your Illusion* by Guns N' Roses.

We spent ages trying to come up with a headline for the Nirvana review, but with a deadline looming settled for the faintly obvious 'NEVERMIND – THE BOLLOX'! Still, that's effectively what the piece said. It's odd re-reading it now. But here's some of it:

> Nirvana do here what Sonic Youth did so emphatically with *Goo* last year – making the move from cult indie to major label with not so much as a hiccup. In fact, just as the Sonics impressed and outstripped the sceptics' expectations, Nirvana have made an LP which is not only better than anything they've done before, it'll stand up as a new reference point for the future post-hardcore generation.
>
> *Nevermind* is a record for people who'd like to like Metallica, but can't stomach their lack of melody; while on the other hand it takes some of the Pixies' nous with tunes and gives the idea new muscle. A shock to the system. Tracks like the excellent 'In Bloom' and best of the lot 'Come As You

Are' show a dexterity that combines both a tension and laid-back vibe that work off each other to produce some cool, constructed twists and turns.

Nevermind is the big American alternative record of the autumn. (9 out of 10).

I nicked the line about Metallica from fellow *NME* scribe Mary Anne Hobbs (now a fellow 6 Music DJ). Mary Anne had come from *Sounds* and was shrewd and opinionated. She was another great ally – and hard to beat in an argument. She got the unenviable task of writing our first Nirvana cover – just as the band began to suffer under the pressure of their new-found fame.

Our late arrival to Nirvana might not have been spot on, but the timing of their arrival to a bigger, broader audience was pretty much impeccable. You could see *Nevermind* as an antidote to Madchester, the post-baggy sounds of the Scream, *and* to the slower, more insular music of Britain's shoe-gazing bands such as Chapterhouse and Slowdive. In fact, Chapterhouse were never the same again after having to follow Nirvana on the main stage at the Reading Festival that year.

NME finally put them on the cover in November 1991. Kurt had to be gently persuaded to do the photos by his press officer, but still retaliated with "Look, I'll do the fucking pictures, but after that I just want to be left alone." Despite being slightly reticent to begin with, Mary Anne got a good piece out of them (including the fact that 'Polly', one of the most harrowing songs on the album, was based on a true story and how Krist was worried about a backlash from their original fans now Nirvana were officially big time).

The feature also followed them to the after-the-pub TV hellhole of *The Word*. Kurt swore live on telly and Nirvana did 'Smells Like Teen Spirit' and, two and a half minutes into their performance, the programme rolled the end credits.

But here's the crux of Maz's piece:

Nirvana have made a more profound impact on America with *Nevermind* than Guns N' Roses did with *Appetite For*

Destruction. And they're running all the 'smack and fanny' barons out of town. The fantastic truth about Nirvana's new-found fortune is that there was no prior plan, no strategic media massage, no radio ass-kissing, no trading fine Columbian for favours. Nirvana have made it simply on the magnificent quality of their sound-bytes.

That was the real point of it all. Where the Pistols had failed, Nirvana had succeeded. This was punk rock come to America, 15 years after it started bringing down the dinosaurs in Britain.

Nevermind was culturally important in several ways, but two were particularly pleasing. They all but ended the reign of the poodle rocksters in Spandex trousers who had represented rock music since prehistoric times. I think that's fair.

And they brought to a conclusion the first era of hardcore, from its birth in the underground to its passing-out party at number one in the charts. It had been a long, difficult journey. Hüsker Dü had helped start the ball rolling by metamorphosing from a 30-second thrash band into a gorgeously melodic punk rock group – and signing to Warner Brothers in the process. How shocking was that at the time? I mean, Hüsker Dü were loud, but you could still barely hear them over the cries of sell-out across America.

But Hüsker Dü hadn't sold out. And they made *Candy Apple Grey* and *Warehouse: Songs And Stories*, and though they didn't sell in earth-shattering numbers, they helped create a better atmosphere for bands to make the jump from an indie label to a major. As a result, Sonic Youth joined Geffen. Then Sonic Youth recommended that Geffen sign Nirvana. Nirvana made *Nevermind.*

The trio's success also coincided with – and contributed to – a change in policy among American TV and radio stations, which finally began to embrace alternative pop culture. They were a gift for MTV. They helped reinvent alt-rock radio, which had been surviving on bands like The Cure for years. And they sent out a message to the major labels that a new sort of rock music had arrived.

Of course, having opened the doors to the underground, the American punk scene would never be the same again (or at least it would take some time to recover). The spotlight shone on the best AND the worst bands of the time. And for a lot of people who treasured the very underground nature of grunge and punk it was difficult to watch it being turned into a designer youth culture, with double-page supplement spreads on Slackers and Generation X.

It was a very different world to that of the dodgy compilation tapes of TSOL.

I saw Nirvana a couple more times after *Nevermind*, but by then they were leaving my orbit for bigger things. One of the nights was my friend Tall Graham's stag night – when I had to chaperone various drunkards round the Kilburn National. But Nirvana responded to the big occasion by being at their most ferocious and committed. The crowd, swelled by the success of 'Smells Like Teen Spirit', were wide-eyed and full-on. And really, that seemed as good a point as any to wish them on their way, and to return to the Falcon.

CHAPTER 12

What You Do To Me

Writing for the music press back in the early nineties could be a really good life. You got sent free records and packed off on trips abroad to interview bands and you got invited to dreadful after-show parties. You saw the best and worst of the music biz's excess and met groups who couldn't string four sentences together but had had a college radio hit in the States.

But best of all for me, it meant being able to go to a lot of gigs and see a lot of bands. This required very little skill. Stamina yes, but skill no. The year after I saw 197 gigs I had a bet with fellow journalist Mick Mercer over which of us could be the first to see 200 gigs the following year. I started well, but faded and only did about 170. Mick ran out of cash before he ran out of energy. Yet on certain nights it provides me with such a rush of adrenalin that I can barely sleep at night.

I've always liked finding new groups. It doesn't make me better than anyone else (in fact, it often used to make me far worse, like a stressed teenager at exam time). But I like the challenge. It's not a hair-shirt thing. I enjoy going to small gigs by new bands who are raw and nervous and naive and sometimes – just occasionally – exceptional.

It's not a high ratio – 1:40 for a 'change your world' experience, maybe; 1:4 for a really good night. But the gigs in-between only serve to heighten the anticipation of the great ones. So, the way I look at it, I owe certain venues and promoters a debt of gratitude for their service. After all, it's not easy putting on gigs at the bottom level. I once saw an angry promoter chase a band down the street after they had sneaked out without explaining their failure to bring the promised coachload of fans with them. Brilliantly, she was still carrying her glass of red wine at the time.

I know I'm guilty at times of donning the rose-tinted specs and romanticising about what, let's face it, are mainly just pubs with two rooms or old social clubs. But I think they've got character. People who use the term 'the toilet circuit' as a derogatory description of these venues – ones that hold 250 people or fewer – aren't looking at them in the same way as I do. They're my home turf.

Fortunately, attitudes have started to change over the past decade. The disparaging toilet remarks have been replaced by the more respectful phrase 'grassroots venues' – and the more of them that shut, the more people seem to be waking up to the valuable role they play, not just in nurturing bands in their early days but also more broadly in the local community. For my part, last year I became a patron of the Music Venue Trust, an organisation set up to protect and support small venues around the UK.

Still, I'm not mad enough to say I like everything about them. But I put up with the downsides because I'd rather see a group that's highly charged and fresh than sit in row Z at Wembley Arena watching a band slickly going through their show from afar.

I am not anti-glamour, or anti-big gig, though until recently I was anti-sitting down. I had a furious run-in once with a security man at an Orchestral Manoeuvres gig at the Hammersmith Odeon who wouldn't let me stand at the back rather than sit in my allotted seat. I can only apologise to him now. My friend Simon, meanwhile, has had some very testing times at seated venues. At a Chris Rea gig (why *NME* made him review Chris Rea, I really don't know, but there you go), he was sat next to a family who, between the support act and Rea himself, unpacked a picnic in row G with sandwiches and a flask of tea.

It might just be me, but standing shoulder to shoulder watching a band, when the crowd turns into one writhing mass… it represents a kind of odd unity. Trying to hold yourself upright, craning your neck for a better view, it's somehow easier to lose yourself in the whole gig experience.

Sitting down, I feel more alone or part of a smaller picture (and for certain gigs where you want a one-to-one with the band, that's absolutely fine). But I'd rather stand anonymously in the throng in an away end watching Colchester United – one part of a bigger entity – than sit at a Manchester United game. And I'd rather feel part of a crowd that shouts as one for an encore than be in an audience which is full of lone voices.

So I'm not anti-big per se. I'm not someone who shouts sell-out at a group who've progressed to stadium level. And I'm no longer the sort of person who thinks bands should pay their dues before getting a whiff of success (though paying their dues makes for more romantic copy). I just like all this.

Here's a couple of reasons why. One night I'd gone to the Falcon in Camden, then the Phil Kaufman Club, run by Jeff Barrett. It was a Saturday, so I'd stopped off to buy some comics en route, before taking up a position at the corner of the bar with the latest issues of *Daredevil* and *Hellblazer*.

The headline band, who I was there to review, were called The Caretaker Race, but Barrett – who used to book the bands and man the door – popped out from the back room and starting raving about the support band. Incredible singer. Only their third gig. How many more sweet nothings can a journalist take?

So I fell for it, and I ventured into the back room. And for once it very nearly *was* like walking through the back of the wardrobe into Narnia. There in the orangey light – the Falcon was lit by a single lightbulb at the time – were The Sundays: gorgeous, angelic and chilling. The Caretaker Race never stood a chance after that. The Sundays went on to become the next big thing and 'Can't Be Sure', their debut single, was number one in John Peel's Festive 50 in 1989. And I smile at this, because once again I happened to be in the right place at the right time.

Other bands you have to persist with more. Just over a year later, a tape turned up at *NME* of a Scottish group called Teenage Fanclub which was absolutely show-stopping. It was effortless and melodic and garagey and West Coast. It really was a lovely thing.

The Fanclub were due to play their first two London shows over the same weekend, starting with the Falcon on the Friday night. Unbeknownst to the audience, though, the group had started drinking as soon as they'd got in their van in Glasgow. And by the time they arrived for the soundcheck they were already a bit merry.

The set was a drunken shambles. Brilliant. But an utter shambles. Halfway through the set, as another potential gem of a song stuttered to a halt for the second time, their singer Norman Blake asked the audience: "Do you want us to have another go at this one, or go on to another one. Hands up for this one..." And so it went on. The following night in the dungeonesque basement bar of the White Horse in Hampstead (no stage, so you had to grab a chair to stand on to see them), they were sober and terrific. And I remember looking around the room, and everyone was thinking the same thing. There was a collective glint in the audience's eye, and it's at those times that you realise you're caught up in something special.

I could go on with stories like this all night – like the neighbour with too many holiday snapshots – but you get the picture. You know. You know because it's happened to you as well. In a venue or in a tent in a field – the moment of almost inexplicable joy. A moment that will always live with you.

OK, there's possibly something worrying about the fact that I have been going to the 100 Club for 35 years (that's effectively seven comprehensive school educations). And I haven't grown up or learned anything much.

All I know now is that if a band says they're on at nine, then they mean 9.15; that all bands from St Albans bring a coachload of fans with them; and that at at least one in three gigs I will get stuck behind The Tall Man or The Snogging Couple.

But hats off to the grassroots venues: from Glasgow to Manchester; from the Southampton Joiners to Cardiff's Clwb Ifor Bach to the Hull Adelphi. And, lest we forget them, to the ones we've lost, like the Bull and Gate, the Falcon and... the Oval Cricketers.

CHAPTER 13

(Kennington) Parklife

The Oval Cricketers was a single, rectangular box room of a pub, an averagely uninviting oblong, situated two minutes' walk from the Oval cricket ground. But I have fond affection for the Cricketers because of two nights I spent propping up the bar there.

The first was three days after I came out of hospital. I'd been rushed in a fortnight earlier suffering from the double whammy of septic tonsillitis and glandular fever, which had come as a bit of a shock (as you naturally assume you are indestructible in your twenties).

I still give the whole episode some romantic topspin, though, when I bore people with the story these days. I was thrown in an ambulance and arrived in hospital with medics running around looking worried and whispering under their breath. That sort of thing. I've even managed to persuade some listeners that I kept the ambulance waiting while I wrote the final paragraph of a feature that had to be handed in the next day for *NME*. But there is some truth in all this.

One evening, as my throat had started seizing up, I was working on a piece about a Welsh band called The Darling Buds. By the time I'd got to the end of the article, I found that swallowing had become a serious problem, and that's when I eventually gave in. I got a lift to St Thomas's Hospital (again) where a doctor shone a torch in my mouth and said, resignedly, "If you could see your tonsils now, they'd make you want to puke."

After a week on a drip, the medical team finally said they would release me when I could prove to them that I could eat again. The next morning they gave me a bowl of Bran Flakes for breakfast. It was like eating razorblades, but it got me to the front door.

"Complete rest," said the doctor, waving me out of the ward.

"Completely impossible," I never bothered replying.

After getting home to find that one of the goldfish had died, I sat around for two days watching TV before I could take it no longer. Glandular fever is bad, but back then gig withdrawal was worse. I'd get fidgety and grouchy and pad round the house without purpose. So that's how I ended up at the Cricketers to see Senseless Things bash through their Fraggle Rock set while I took up drinking again.

It's the other trip to the Cricketers, though, that's the important one. On the other occasion I saw Blur. They weren't called Blur at that point and they didn't sound much like the Blur people know now, but it really was them. As with many bands I've gone to see in my time, Seymour had come via a tip-off – in this case from a guy called Simon, who balanced working in the *NME* ad department with playing in a band called Vicious Kiss. The Kiss had just appeared at another dimly lit London venue, the Sir George Robey in Finsbury Park. Simon phoned a couple of days later and said: "You should go and see the band we played with… Seymour. I didn't like them much, but they're good at what they do."

Having tracked down a management company phone number, I got a tape and a list of gigs and then trolled off to see them (checking an old diary, it was December 12, 1989, with a scribbled note next to it adding "On at 8.45 p.m."). The great thing about the Cricketers was that it was only about a mile away on the 133 bus from where I was living in Brixton. So if the band were rubbish, you could be home in 15 minutes. But Seymour weren't rubbish. They weren't anything like I'd expected either. Or, to be more precise, they didn't fit in anywhere – apart from sounding oddly at times like angular C86 band The Wolfhounds.

Cramped on the stage – which was about six inches high and covered in gaffer tape – the four boys part bounced, part sulked through a set which was more intriguing than convincing. The singer hurled himself around and bumped into the guitarist, who then looked annoyed. Meanwhile the bassist loafed about in the corner smoking cigarettes. One of them – I'm pretty sure it was Graham – wore a blue-and-white hooped T-shirt, the sort that turned up again in one of the band's early photoshoots. It was all very confusing.

Among the rest of the audience that night – a small crowd of about 80 people – were Andy Ross and Dave Balfe from Food Records who had been on the band's trail for a couple of months already. Food eventually signed Seymour in March 1990, prompting the change of name to Blur and a fresh assault on the London gig circuit. I'm sure this is my memory playing tricks on me, but they must have played the Bull and Gate three times in six weeks during the run-up to the release of their first single, 'She's So High'.

I did my first interview with them at the start of October 1991, to coincide with the single's release, and I've followed them ever since. And this is why they have a special place in this book: because Blur are probably the one band that I feel I've grown up with. I suppose it helps that we're around the same age and that three of them grew up in Colchester, near where I lived. But also their career has oddly mirrored my own ups and downs (we were both new kids on the block in 1989, we were both out of favour in 1992, both back in favour again in 1994, and both reinventing ourselves by 1997).

We conducted the first interview back in Colchester, which on reflection was a weird choice because none of us had a good thing to say about the place at the time. I've since made my peace with Colchester. (There is the football club, of course, and we did an *Evening Session* show there with Ash at the Arts Centre – dubbed 'Return Of Lamacq' – which is still one of my favourite nights of the nineties. Tickets sold out in 26 minutes. I was speechless.) But, at the time, the town was a painful memory of squaddies and apathy and no gigs and goths in the city centre.

I described Colchester's demeanour as 'smart casual', but Graham Coxon was even bleaker: "When I was at school we were asked to bring in photos of what people thought of Colchester. And everyone just brought in pictures of men digging holes."

Damon, though, did tell a great story about how his school had burned down seven times in two years. Police eventually found that the arsonist was… one of the teachers.

"And he was still there at the time," he added. "Burning down the school at night and then coming in the next day and saying, 'Sorry children, someone has set fire to the school again, so we're going to have to move to another building.'"

The setting for the interview was the Hole In The Wall pub (so named because it sits beside the Roman wall). Most of Colchester's alternative and student crowd spent time in the Hole. Not many of them copied Blur and drank halves of cider and Pernod.

Damon: "Fifteen of these and I'm away."

The photo session followed in Colchester Castle Park, under the willow trees by the boating lake. It really was the calm before the storm. Apart from the misguided return to Colchester, Blur were in the right place at the right time. As Madchester's momentum gained pace, they were one of the few bands from around London who showed hit potential – and they were good looking and articulate. Damon sounded assured and informed: "There are fundamental reasons why people like bands. They're drawn to them because they WANT them – whether it's in an emotional, sexual or intellectual way, they want that band. That's us."

The next 18 months you might possibly know. 'She's So High' was followed by 'There's No Other Way', which I've never really liked that much. It was a floppy version of Blur, which was right for the time, I suppose, but it's become an in-joke between Damon Albarn and me that I get the wrong sort of chill every time I hear it now.

Still, it did the trick for them, going Top 10 in 1991. Then came the *Smash Hits* photoshoots and the debut album *Leisure*, which received a mixed reaction. They didn't help themselves much by following the LP with 'Bang', a single that managed to sweep the board by *not working on any level whatsoever* (critically, commercially, you name it, 'Bang' flunked it).

But the worst failing of 'Bang' was that, once again, it didn't capture the pure abandon of Blur's live gigs. If they had a real problem at the end of 1991 it was with perception. To the casual observer Blur were just a bunch of southern middle-class idiots who'd had a big teen hit and spent the rest of the year on the razzle (they'd hit the jealousy jackpot with 'There's No Other Way'). And what else? The singer was arrogant, the rest of them were drunk, and their songs didn't stand up to a second listen. In a strangely prescient conversation with Creation boss Alan McGee, he told me that summer: "They're nice blokes but they've got no songs."

In fact they had quite a few good songs, but *Leisure* didn't sound emphatic enough to properly showcase them. Their gigs, on the other hand, were something else. Damon said around this time that if he didn't feel ill at the end of a gig then it couldn't have been that great a show. The singer, with more room to play with than at the Oval Cricketers, used to look like he'd just plugged himself into a light socket: he'd hang from the ceiling, charge round the stage, and in extreme cases throw himself off the PA stack. The band, meanwhile, made a far thicker and fuller noise than the album suggested.

Their last live performance of 1991 was typical of all this. They played the Food Records' Christmas party at London's Brixton Academy with labelmates Jesus Jones, Whirlpool and Sensitise and stole the show. Christmas and New Year is always a time for reflection, but Blur had more to think about than most (after all, they'd been through the whole rise and fall of a pop band in less than 18 months). Upstairs in the bar afterwards, Damon seemed a little subdued, though he did introduce me to his mum and dad who were there.

We were just making plans to maybe meet up in the Hole a couple of days before Christmas when his mum turned round and said: "Damon, don't forget you've got carol singing that night."

And that was that. I didn't see him at Christmas. I didn't see any of them for ages.

Have you ever heard the theory of consensus terrorism? OK, here's an example. Blur hadn't retired to Colchester, hiding their faces in shame after a particularly lousy version of 'We Three Kings'. They'd actually gone away and made what I still think is one of their best singles – the boisterous, slightly punky 'Pop Scene'.

It should have been the record that revived not only their chart career but their credibility rating too. It was the first that went close to capturing the immediacy of their live shows – but it still had a brass section to give it a hint of polish. But the record was cursed from the word go. Parlophone, Food's parent label, disagreed over the choice of video edit (the better, Food-favoured version is the one with subtitles of the lyrics flashing up at the bottom of the screen). Then there was the reaction from the media hipsters and tastemakers.

Now, it was Damon who came up with the concept of consensus terrorism, and I wouldn't be surprised if he didn't find it forming in his head around the release of 'Pop Scene'. This is roughly how it works.

Tastemaker A hears the record and decides that he or she doesn't like it, or it doesn't fit into the musical climate of the time. Then Tastemaker B, who has been sitting on the fence, agrees. Tastemaker C, probably junior to the other two, goes along with them.

You now have three people – who wield some sort of importance – all against you, even though a couple of them couldn't really care less either way. But if you think that's bad, that's just the start. When their friends – who haven't even heard the record yet – ask what it's like, they're told it's not much cop. They nod, and to join in they say, "Oh, I always thought they'd blow it," and they leave with their opinion: your record's rubbish. That night at a gig, when somebody else asks them about the single, they pass the criticism on: "Oh, it's rank." Have you heard it? "No, but everyone who has says it's really weak." You are now officially ALL OVER.

And I know that the machinations of the media are more complex than this – and that one bad case of Chinese whispers can't be held entirely responsible for the destruction of a group's career. But I've seen consensus terrorism in action (even been a part of it on occasion), and it does undermine people's confidence in a group.

So Blur found themselves in a spot of bother. The consensus view was that, despite the record's eager, edgy, excitable sound, they were going to struggle in 1992. Grunge had arrived, and the home counties bands who'd been into baggy and shoe-gazing were about to be swept aside. 'Pop Scene' scrabbled to 32 in the chart (eight places lower than 'Bang') and that was the proof that the doubters needed. Blur had blown it.

I don't know where I was when *Modern Life Is Rubbish* was released. I might have been on tour. I know I was working as freelance reviews editor at *Select*, but *Modern Life* snuck into the shops while I wasn't looking. It took me a couple of months to catch up with their new mod style and their more classic take on British pop. But already you could feel the pendulum swinging back in favour of the British bands through 1993, and *Select* – particularly the astute David Cavanagh – was quick off the mark in spotting the potential in *Modern Life*.

They weren't the only ones. Over at Radio 1, Blur recorded two sessions for Mark Goodier's *Evening Session* in fairly quick succession. The second, in April 1993, featured early versions of two of the tracks that would make it onto the next album, *Parklife* ('Bank Holiday' and a curious version of the title track with Damon singing the lines later handled by Phil Daniels).

The *Session*'s support meant that by the time Jo Whiley and I arrived, we were guaranteed the first play of 'Girls And Boys'. I think we were both a bit bewildered by it (I think I even mentioned that it reminded me of Human League). What was this disco romp? This cheery singalong? This wasn't *Modern Life*. It was only when advance copies of the album arrived that the new material began to make sense.

As a result, I interviewed Blur in the cramped overnight studios at Radio 1's old Egton House building and we made a big thing of *Parklife*. The reaction to the record was astonishingly good. Food label boss Andy Ross has since claimed that the good reviews were so over the top because critics felt they'd missed the boat on *Modern Life* (which by now was a great cult record). But *Parklife* was a stylish and well-executed record in its own right.

TRIVIA FACT: The album very nearly wasn't called *Parklife*. Damon revealed to us in 1999 that the sleeve was originally going to feature a fruit and veg stall. And, at the suggestion of Food's then other half Dave Balfe, it was going to be called *London*. I mean, gawd bless you guv, but *London*? LONDON!

By a stroke of luck, just before the album's release Radio 1 took the *Session* off air, the night the *Parklife* tour was due to start (there was an Amnesty International concert aired in the show's place). So, on the spur of the moment, I took a train to Nottingham Rock City with a DAT machine and filed an opening night review – including reaction from the band and an interview with the support group Sleeper. The *Session* worked well as a duo at the time, because a couple of weeks later to balance things up, Jo did a similar roving report on Oasis, on the night Liam Gallagher was thumped by a disgruntled punter at Newcastle Riverside.

No one got thumped at Rock City. Blur simply went on and had the crowd in their pockets from the word go. Before they played the Mile End Stadium at the height of *Parklife* fever, this was the most celebratory gig I'd ever seen them do.

I suppose that given our history and my geographical bias, I'd always end up on Blur's side if there was a war between the two groups. But even so, in the week that Oasis and Blur went head to head in a race for the number one slot, I bought a copy of each of their singles (the live CD of 'Country House' and a seven-inch of 'Roll With It'). The tabloid press were finding it hard to pick a side too. But there were stories every day in *The Sun* and *The Mirror*, and the rest of the national papers leapt on the story as well. I'd seen the press put pop on the front page before (whether it was the *Daily Star* calling for Snoop Doggy Dogg to be thrown out of the country or 'The Secret Lives Of Socialist Pop Band The Housemartins'). But there had been nothing as lasting and concerted as this. Britpop was part of the nation's fabric now.

As the sales figures started to filter through with two days to go, no one wanted to tempt fate. But the Blur camp organised a 'celebration' party anyway at a private club called Soho House, so I guess they must have been reasonably confident. I got an invite, and turned up on the Sunday evening, a couple of hours after they'd officially been announced as the new number one. The atmosphere was strange. All the faces were there: Andy Ross and Miles Jacobson, his A&R man at Food (who would later go on to run the massively popular computer game Championship Manager), the Parlophone press office, some regulars from the Good Mixer and assorted friends. But it was hard to work out exactly what we were all celebrating. Was it Blur at number one? Or was it the fact that, temporarily, Oasis were number two?

Don't get me wrong. It was a nice do, and there were smiles all round, but, if anything, the conflict with Oasis had distracted people from the better story – Blur. The band who were all over two years previously were at number one.

The slightly strained atmosphere continued as Graham Coxon got drunk and then tried climbing out of the second-storey window of the bar. As someone grabbed his legs and hauled him back in (Graham trying to wriggle free the whole time), I thought that it was a good time to leave.

I'm aware that at some points in this book, I'm probably telling you what you already know. For instance, the post-'Country House' history of the two bands has been pretty well documented. Damon gave a rather cocky interview to *Q* magazine about the relative merits and popularity of the two groups. But within a year he was eating his words as Oasis stole the show in the UK and then found further success in the States. To coin the obvious phrase: Blur had won the first battle, but it was Oasis who were winning the war.

And again, I saw a comparison between Blur and myself. Apart from his post-number one crowing, it felt for much of this period as if Blur had been drawn into a competition they didn't particularly want or need. I think it gave them a sort of personality crisis.

They began to lose track of what the band stood for (was it a type of music, or was it how many gold discs they had compared with the boys down the road?). At Radio 1 I found myself slipping into the same frame of mind. The obvious comparison would be to cast Jo Whiley as Oasis and me as Blur. But that doesn't work. It suggests that Jo's success was something I resented or couldn't handle, whereas, to be honest, deep down, I was really pleased for her. When she won the prestigious Sony Award for Best DJ, I confess I had a tear in my eye.

No, the problem was that Jo – who landed her own programme on Saturdays and then the lunchtime show and TV – was doing loads of stuff and I thought I should be too. I didn't want to do TV, or be a daytime DJ, but I became preoccupied with the notion of a rat race, that I needed to raise my profile and not get left behind. If every other Radio 1 DJ is doing television, then I should be doing it too. It was a ridiculous mindset. It also made me extraordinarily unhappy.

And I don't exactly know when it changed. But sometime, just as Blur stopped worrying about being the biggest band in Britain and went back to making records they enjoyed, I stopped arguing over how many times our show was trailed on air and went back to being a bloke who loves playing records for a living. All the clutter went in the bin. It was great.

Meanwhile, extricated from the war with Oasis, Blur found a new freedom that resulted first in *Blur* and then *13*. And ironically, as they stopped trying so hard to make hit records, they came up with one of their most successful tunes ever, 'Song 2'. I saw them play all their singles in order on tour at Christmas 1999 in Brighton (couldn't bear the thought of going to Wembley). And nearly every track has a memory attached to it now. No wonder Damon started writing movie soundtracks – because inadvertently he's been writing one for me for over 25 years.

Mind you, I still had to go to the bar during 'There's No Other Way'.

CHAPTER 14

Teethgrinder

Chronologically, this is a difficult part of the story to fit in, but in October 1992 my career at *NME* ended as quickly and almost as ridiculously as it had started. Our leader and spiritual mentor Danny Kelly announced his imminent departure to join *Q* magazine, and the paper duly advertised for a new editor.

It's hard to put my finger on exactly what happened next. I think the paper's publishers, IPC, knew who they wanted as their next editor. But they interviewed some of the staff anyway – me included. However, after a fortnight without any of us hearing anything, the rumour mill went into overdrive. The new editor was coming from our sworn rivals the *Melody Maker*. There were big changes afoot.

To be honest, I couldn't see myself working with the new boss. In fact, I couldn't see where I was going at *NME* at all. There was talk at the time that the paper wanted to enlarge its news coverage at the expense of championing new bands. And if that was the case, what was the point of being there? I took the only sensible route out of the situation. I ran away.

On the day the news broke, Alan Lewis spent the morning informing staff that the new editor would be officially announced at midday. In what can only be described as a fit of pique, I left his office, wrote my letter of resignation and went to the pub. At the High Noon meeting, various members of staff expressed their dismay at the decision. And then, as we filed out, I handed in my notice to quit. Bless her, just a step behind me was Mary Anne Hobbs handing in her resignation as well.

I was sad and angry and confused at the time. And there were days when I was working out my notice when I worried if I was doing the right thing. But in the end, leaving *NME* was the best move I'd made since joining it. I'd done my time. It was good fun and it made me happy and insanely annoyed all at the same time. But it was good to get out. I was £500 overdrawn and I didn't know what I was going to do next, but hey, £500 for five years of free records and guest lists and a job that didn't start till 10.30 in the morning. That's not bad value.

In the uneasy weeks that formed my period of notice, I had a couple of final features to write. Amazingly, having missed out on various jaunts to the States over the past year, I was sent there twice in the space of a fortnight. The first was to interview Therapy? for their debut cover story in New York – a trip which coincided with my birthday. I flew out with their press officer, Andy, and photographer Kevin Cummins, and we met the band on the first night in some Irish bar near Greenwich Village.

Meeting bands you're going to interview for the first time is strange. There's usually a period of polite conversation as you form your initial impressions of each other. Then generally the atmosphere becomes more relaxed (unless you've really messed up or dropped a huge clanger, in which case you can feel the air chilling around you).

Therapy? turned out to be one of the nicest bunches of blokes I'd met in ages. We worked out that because of the time difference it was already my birthday in England, so they bought a huge round of drinks and we started celebrating. It was a relief to be away from London. An hour into the first session, they introduced me to their latest favourite pub challenge: Whose Round Is It Anyway? Contestants (i.e. whoever was buying the drinks) had to walk to and from the bar in the style of a chosen celebrity or pop star nominated by the rest of the table. Bassist Michael unluckily got Gary Numan.

If I was going to miss anything about the *NME*, it wasn't going to be raging debates over the future of pop, or finishing another singles page at 3 a.m., or even the free tickets to gigs. What I was going to miss was watching the bassist of Ireland's premier new rock trio jerkily making his way back to our table impersonating a robot.

CHAPTER 15

Waking Up

I might have been broke when I left the *NME* – the unfortunate result of a reliance on black cabs and an ever deepening pinball habit – but I left with a lot of stories to tell. Not all of them mine. One of my favourites was actually recounted to me by a fellow journalist at the paper, after he'd returned from doing an interview for the arts section of the paper. (Spoiler alert: If you're thinking of coming to one of my one-man shows, then maybe skip this next part, because it's one of the 'highlights' of the evening.)

So there are two cultural scientists and they want to find out more about our basic attitudes to consumerism. Is there something in the human psyche that draws us to certain designs or materials? To do this, they borrow a monkey, and the monkey sits on a stool while they hand it various objects.

The monkey's reactions – they argue – will tell us a lot about our gut instincts, our primal urges.

Halfway through the experiment they hand the monkey a CD. Not the case, just the CD. The monkey looks at its reflection, looks bored and then throws it to the floor. Then they give it a 12-inch single. The monkey holds it and looks at it. And then... the monkey gets a hard-on.

I'm not sure what this says about the human race, but I've ended up using this story to try to win all types of arguments – especially when I was trying to run a record label of my own. In fact, it would probably be easier to explain the monkey story than it is to explain how a tiny indie label ended up having a number one album and putting Annie Lennox's nose out of joint in the process. But here goes.

During my days at *NME* I met and got to know a Liverpudlian PR man called Alan James. James looked after a series of struggling indie bands in his early days, and I suspect I was one of the few people who would talk to him. In return, he was the only PR man who ever sent me records.

What finally helped Alan make the grade as a PR, though, was not his growing roster of bands and his ability to squeeze even the worst of them into the pages of the press. It was his unfathomable vocabulary and phraseology. For instance: if Alan thought somebody was a bit flaky, then this person became 'a man of egg'. If they were guilty of more series crimes against pop they were 'a man of ham'. As we started questioning his sanity further, James's vocal dexterity became more and more bizarre.

One day I answered the phone on the live desk and all I heard from the other end was: "It's like chicken and cheese pies with no cheese in" (you probably need to say this in a thinly worn Scouse accent for maximum impact). He treated us to some amazing outbursts in his time, but this is still my favourite.

This is his description of a band's piss-poor new single: "It's like a piece of ham sliding down a blue bucket... but, wait, wait... the bucket's got holes in."

We shared contempt for certain major labels and the way they frittered money away on unsalvageable bands. And inevitably we vowed that one day we'd start a label together and show them what for. And inevitably we spent years studiously doing nothing about it. In the end, Deceptive Records happened almost by accident.

In November 1992, having walked out of the *NME*, I found myself back in Harlow, bored and broke. Sitting in the downstairs bar of the town's only venue, the Square, a friend wandered up and said: "Anthony Chapman was looking for you the other day. He's got a tape of his new band he wants you to have." Big Ant had been in, or championed, various squawky lo-fi bands in the area, including the ill-fated local heroes Pregnant Neck, and had gone on to experiment with dance music. Two minutes later, by complete chance, he walked in clutching a demo of his latest outfit, Collapsed Lung.

The Lung demo was a roughshod mix of guitars and hip-hop and tongue-in-cheek lyrics. It was also, I determinedly persuaded myself, fate telling me that now was the time I should start this label. Which is how come Alan James and I, with A&R man Tony Smith, came to launch Deceptive Records. The label name was nicked from the flexi-disc I'd released with *A Pack Of Lies*; the money, meanwhile, came from Tony and Alan's bank accounts.

Deceptive was set up for roughly £3,000 and given an office above Alan James PR in a rickety building near the Elephant and Castle. The front door always used to stick and then you had to climb a couple of flights of stairs that were perennially littered with boxes left outside by the T-shirt company with which James shared the first floor.

When Deceptive released its first single, the one-room office consisted of a chair, two phones, a desk and an old filing cabinet. When people wanted to come round for meetings, Tony, in a deadpan voice, used to say: "Four o'clock's fine but can you bring your own chair?" Mostly, if we did want to have a meeting we used to go to the Heavy Metal pub on the corner (so named because it used to run a weekly Rock Nite and because the jukebox would – apparently of its own accord – suddenly burst into action every 15 minutes playing a Guns N' Roses epic at searing volume. You could set your watch by that jukebox).

The first release was Collapsed Lung's debut single, 'Thundersley Invacar', which sold out of its initial 3,000 pressing and was played on Jackie Brambles' lunchtime show on Radio 1. It got to something like 108 in the chart. By this point, I'd started work at *Select* magazine and had to juggle phone calls from penniless freelancers with desperate messages about sleeve artwork (the designer John Anonymous would phone and talk about cromalins and I would sit on the other end of the line and listen until I got a headache).

It was via *Select*, however, that I met Elastica. Stuart Maconie had been to interview some new band which featured Damon Albarn's girlfriend Justine Frischmann – and she'd asked Stuart to see if Deceptive might be interested in meeting up and talking about a single. I had no idea who they were, but within two weeks it seemed that everyone was raving about them. I got hold of their demo from somewhere and heard 'Vaseline' and thought it sounded a little bit like early Blondie (I come from a generation of boys who had instantly fallen for Blondie, not just for the breathless pop they used to release but also for the black-and-white pin-ups of Debbie Harry and her effortless, just-got-out-of-bed cool).

Elastica, to me, had a different yet equally endearing look. When the pictures for their feature arrived in the *Select* office, they looked like they'd shopped from a similar catalogue (or charity shop) to the one Blur had used for *Modern Life Is Rubbish* – but instead of the smart old-school mod image, Elastica looked like the Bash Street Kids. They looked brilliant.

Having missed two low-key gigs outside London, my first chance to see them was at the Falcon in Camden. Although when I say 'see *them*', I mean see some of them. The back room was so full that I got wedged by the PA and consequently spent the gig going deaf in one ear, while craning my neck to catch sight of anything that moved. I saw singer Justine and bassist Annie, and I think I caught a glimpse of Donna's guitar, but that was it.

I met Justine for the first time one afternoon in the West End pub the Spice Of Life, just off Cambridge Circus. I have no idea why we picked this place. Justine claims it was my idea, but quite how taking her to a pub full of tourists and businessmen and frazzled West End shoppers was going to endear me to the new Debbie Harry, I really don't know.

Anyway, it transpired that various labels had already expressed an interest in Elastica, but Justine was wary of signing to a major because of the control they could exert over the band. As selling points go, I didn't have much to retaliate with (I was wondering how to break it to her that Deceptive was one chair and two phones). Instead, I waffled on about formatting being the work of the devil and wanting to make a record that had all the excitement of 'Teenage Kicks'.

And then I did the monkey story.

I'm not sure if it was the monkey story that did the trick, but Justine organised a meeting with the rest of the group. In the meantime, having demoed material for Mike Smith, the A&R man at EMI Publishing, they finally signed a publishing deal with him in the middle of August. The night started with a meal in the West End, but because the band didn't want to sign on Friday the 13th, they dragged Smith up to Primrose Hill, where they finally put their names on the contract at one minute past midnight. Smith later told me he thought it was all an elaborate hoax, and that come midnight, having got him faintly tipsy, they were simply going to roll him down the hill.

We regrouped in the Good Mixer in Camden and shook hands on a two-single Deceptive deal on August 17. The first single was going to be 'Line Up'. A couple of days later it was going to be 'Vaseline'. And in the end it was 'Stutter' (which I thought was a nice balance between the two, and anyway I think we were all growing bored of the daily discussions over what the single would be – we wanted to get onto the exciting second level of artwork and release dates).

I couldn't get the 'Teenage Kicks' spiel out of my head. It had to be a monkey-friendly sexy seven-inch and it had to be pressed really loud, and it had to have something neat inscribed in the run-out groove. Creation had just released a Sugar single in a brown card sleeve which looked good, so I nicked that idea – and told Justine we should have an illustrated colour label, because that's what The Clash did with '(White Man) In Hammersmith Palais'. Originally, the centre of the record was going to feature a picture of a topless page three model from a set of *Sun* playing cards Justine owned. But nobody could quite ascertain whether *The Sun* would sue us or not – so we opted for plan B, an illustration of Donna. The follow-ups would feature the rest of the band.

The decision to release the first record on seven-inch only wasn't purely a romantic nod to the late seventies, which we all had affection for (me for my early teens, them for their musical influences). As part of our attempts to raise Deceptive's profile, I'd been invited out by a sales rep from the distribution company who had taken me on a tour of shops around Derby and Nottingham. One in particular was fascinating. It was a dance shop in Derby that stocked all the latest house and hip-hop, but also, in a corner, had a rack of independent seven-inches. "We don't touch indie CDS," the guy behind the counter explained, "but we get quite a few customers flicking through those."

We also made the decision to press only 1,000 copies, because, at the time, Elastica were still just a buzz-name on the London circuit and none of us wanted loads of unsold records in bargain bins. In the days of High Street record shops, that surely had to be the most deflating experience for a band. You'd spend months writing and recording and dreaming of the big things to follow, only to end up in a Woolworths bargain bin for 50p. And no matter how much your manager or your friends consoled you with stories about how record shops overstocked on material, that feeling of being unwanted would surely remain. I once read a story about a brilliant little Leeds band called Girls At Our Best who even split up because they couldn't cope with seeing their LP remaindered in their local shop.

In the end, 1,500 copies were made (though as the favourable reviews started to flood in that wasn't nearly enough to cater for the demand). Even the band started phoning up complaining that their mates in Brighton or Newport or Outer Mongolia couldn't get a copy. But by this time, Elastica were big news. There were lots of people who wanted a Debbie Harry who didn't look like Debbie Harry, and there were lots of people who liked the short, sharp pop stabs that were Elastica's forte.

'Line Up' coupled with 'Vaseline' followed as the second single (with the addition of 'Rockunroll' and 'Annie' on the CD). And I know I'm thoroughly biased here, and it was my label and everything, but I'm really very proud of that record. All critical faculties fail me. To celebrate the release of the single they embarked on their first headlining tour and I went up to see them at the Leeds Duchess on the Saturday after the single hit the shops.

There was much discussion on the night over where the record might end up in the chart. Hopefully in the Top 40, maybe even just inside the Top 30. I got the train back to London the next day and listened to Mark Goodier on my Walkman presenting the rundown on Radio 1. By number 29 I was beginning to fidget. He kept playing records and none of them were by Elastica. By the time he introduced number 24 I was convinced that 'Line Up' had charted at 41 and that Deceptive was chicken and cheese pies with no cheese in.

Then honestly this happened.

Goodier: "And at number 20 it's another new entry from one of the most hotly tipped new bands in the countrsshshshshshshshshshshshshshshshshshshshshshsh."

We'd lost the signal as we entered a tunnel just outside Kings Cross. Oh bollocks. Oh God. Is it us? Can't anyone make this train go any quicker?

Eventually the train shunted itself forward, and there was 'Line Up', the last 20 seconds of it. Elastica were a Top 20 band. Elastica were going to be on *Top Of The Pops*.

They were very nervous. The entire 'staff' of Deceptive turned up in their dressing room to give them moral support, but I think we might just have made things worse (three expectant fathers pacing up and down in your dressing room and biting their nails isn't probably what you need just before your biggest TV appearance to date). Justine has also never forgiven me for my pre-show pep talk.

"When the camera gets anywhere near you," I said. "Use your eyes. You've got really good eyes." If you ever get a chance to see a video of the performance, note how Justine stares maniacally into the camera at every close-up. She looks like she's trying to force her eyeballs out of her sockets. It wasn't quite the alluring, sultry effect I was thinking of.

Despite this, the dates sold out and the press ran front covers, and after tedious weeks of arguing over remixes and producers, the album was finished. It was released on March 13, the same week as the latest Annie Lennox album. Lennox was tipped by just about everyone to top the chart, which wasn't surprising because she was famous and had the might of RCA behind her. Elastica had three berks, two phones and still only one chair.

But Elastica had everything else on their side. The album was great. They looked even more like a band now than in the original knockabout gang shots that had first turned up at *Select*. I've still got a picture of them from around the release of the album that's up in my front room. There's the four of them, all dressed in black, and I can't describe how it makes me feel, or what's so great about them and this picture. It just feels RIGHT. Cool isn't quite the word. Nor is sexy. But they have the look of a classic rock'n'roll group. The sort of group who thinks that it's 'us against the world'.

I think that's why the pairing of Elastica and Deceptive worked, particularly in the week the album came out. It really did feel like us against the establishment. What was most touching, though, were the calls that came in during the week from people who'd been out to buy the record and wanted to tell the band and label how great they thought it was. I couldn't even bear to set foot in the office. It was too nerve-wracking. Tony was running the show virtually single-handed, and although I knew about some of the nightmares he was having (Was there enough stock in the shops? Would the massed ranks of the Annie Lennox army descend on Our Price on Saturday and pip Elastica to the post?).

The chart comes through to labels and distributors on a Sunday afternoon. In my more disturbed moments I'd like to change this system and make it more like the announcement of a general election result. Get the Top 5 bands together on a stage and read out their sales figures to the cheers and derision of an invited audience of fans. Believe me, it would be the biggest draw since we put people in the stocks for blowing their nose in a funny way.

Under the existing system, though, we all waited at home for the phone call (after all, there was no way I was going to risk being on public transport this time). Tony phoned at around 4 p.m. "WE'VE BLOODY DONE IT! IT'S NUMBER ONE!"

Not only was it number one, it was the fastest-selling debut album in history. But how do you follow that? I think we all had a few problems coming to terms with Elastica's success. The band was so in demand that they were constantly touring or wrapped up in promotional work. At Deceptive we bought a second chair and a photocopier.

There were difficulties for me, too. By the time the Elastica album went to number one I'd joined Radio 1, and it was a grey area being a DJ and being involved with a record company at the same time. The situation came to a head when head of Radio 1 Trevor Dann was sent two anonymous letters accusing me of bias – and then the *NME* news desk pitched in with claims that I was raking off money from Elastica every time I played them on the radio. This doesn't work as an argument because the cash bands get from radio plays goes through their publishing company – in Elastica's case EMI, not Deceptive – so I wasn't making a penny from the airtime. To be honest, I wasn't making a penny out of the label either, but it became apparent that however much I told people this, there would always be someone who didn't believe me. After a week of mooching around – and, I hate to admit it, feeling unjustly put upon – we got an accountant to draw up some paperwork and I let my share in the company move on for the princely sum of £2.30.

It wasn't just an arbitrary figure. It was the price of a pint of cider in the pub where we concluded the deal. Not exactly Alan McGee stuff, is it? I carried on as a kind of unpaid A&R consultant, bringing in Snuff, Scarfo and the brilliant but underrated Earl Brutus (whose album *Your Majesty... We Are Here* is, I think, one of the best records on the label). But in the end there just weren't enough hours in the day to do everything. And besides, you can't skimp on the day job.

CHAPTER 16

Everything Flows

To explain how I got a job at Radio 1, you have to spin back in time a few years. During my early twenties I'd spent most of my time pursuing some kind of writing career and had had no time for anything as fanciful as DJ ambitions.

So by 1990 my efforts at becoming Somebody Like John Peel hadn't really got very far. My one attempt to break into radio had failed miserably when I was turned down by the local Colchester Hospital radio station for being too young (although I like to think it was because I was too radical for them and their staple diet of Duane Eddy oldies).

In the end, my first steps in radio came without much warning. I took a call one day on the *NME* news desk from a man called Sammy who ranted at length about how the paper was supposed to be clued-up about indie music but didn't even know that London had its own indie pirate radio station. To redress the situation I agreed to meet him outside Manor House Tube station the following Saturday and he'd tell me more.

Sammy arrived, cunningly disguised as the sort of man who promoted seventies disco nights. He then proceeded to drive round in circles for 30 minutes (in order to disguise his route to the studio – apparently blindfolds were out of fashion even then). And finally we pulled up and parked – not outside a tower block or lock-up, but in an anonymous-looking street, somewhere near Leytonstone High Road.

Inside the terraced house, which was, on Saturdays only, Q102's HQ, Sammy explained how he'd started out DJing on the dance pirates and then had a road to Damascus conversion into indie music. Thirty minutes later he shunted me on air for an interview, pronounced my name wrong, and when it was all over said he thought I had a good radio voice. A couple of weeks later he had me doing the late breakfast show from 10 a.m. to midday.

It was both good experience and A Good Experience. The only rules were that the DJs had to pay £10 a week to keep the station on air (generally the money went on new aerials, which either broke or were stolen by rival pirates) and that you never turned up at the house with a record box. You had to disguise your vinyl in carrier bags, and on no account tell anyone where the station was. Of course, the threat of being busted was always there – although Q102 had a novel way of preparing for this possibility. The real owner of the house, a chirpy and no-bullshit fireman, owned two Rottweilers who used to sleep by the front door, just in case the DTI hit squad should turn up one day and break it down. If that happened, added Sammy, DJs were expected to leg it out through the back garden and over the wall (presumably while various members of the DTI were chased back down the High Road, past the kebab shop, by the two pro-pirate hounds).

Deciding to adopt a secret identity, I soon changed my on-air name (for security reasons) and used an old journalistic pseudonym, Andy Hopkirk – inspired by the TV programme *Randall And Hopkirk (Deceased)*. As Andy Hopkirk, I made every mistake that a budding DJ could make: forgetting to close the mic; leaving faders up while I was cueing a track; and, of course, that Peel favourite, playing a record at the wrong speed. But that was nothing in comparison to my near fatal faux pas, which was to spill an entire bottle of Lucozade over the mixing desk, which put the station off air for two weeks. Sammy gave me a very hard time over that.

It was a good time for Q102 though. The DJs were mostly drawn from inside the music industry, and so they brought with them several upfront promos and new releases – which we mixed in with personal favourites.

I naturally assumed that no one could actually hear us, because we were a pirate and our transmitter was probably run on steam. But then we started getting letters of support to the PO Box address, and when the station broke into promotion by staging a gig in Highbury, loads of people turned up. The demand for an alternative guitar station was beginning to become apparent. I had my show extended to three hours and life moved on quite happily. We even broadcast one Christmas Day, when we counted down a listeners' Top 60 all-time favourites (safe in the knowledge that, unless they were on double time, the DTI were at home tucking into their turkey).

But the problem was that Q102 could only go so far. After a couple of years it had achieved all it could as a pirate and it finally fell apart after a heated meeting between backers and presenters held in the front room next to the studio.

However, the foundations that the station had laid didn't go wholly to waste. As Q102 wound up, the campaign for a legal alternative station began, and the London-based XFM was born. Having just got used to not being Someone Like John Peel again, I received a call from Sammy saying we were back on air. XFM was granted its first RSL (a restricted month-long licence) and I was handed the drivetime slot and the Saturday morning alternative chart rundown.

Of the two, the chart was the most exciting programme and the most nerve-wracking. What happened was that the chart itself would be faxed through on a Saturday morning from one of the major Oxford Street shops. We then scanned through it, and if we didn't have some of the records, station all-rounder Frazier had to leg it round the corner to buy them. "And at number 14... I can hear it just coming up the stairs now... hang on a minute..."

My break into mainstream radio came in 1991. I'd met a Radio 1 producer at a meeting to choose bands for a co-sponsored series of Radio 1/*NME* gigs in London. The producer let on that the station was planning a new evening show, to be presented by Mark Goodier, but produced by some chap they'd recruited from Metro Radio in the north-east. "Maybe you should write in and see if they want any help," he suggested.

All I can remember is dashing off a letter which explained my role at the *NME* and that I thought I could give them some tips on bands Radio 1 should be playing (I never was very good at this sort of begging for jobs). A couple of days later the head of music, Roger Lewis, replied and suggested I get in contact with the new man on the block, *Evening Session* producer-to-be Jeff Smith.

It is Smith – alongside Goodier – who did the rest. I took Jeff for a drink one night, ranted and raved about Carter and vowed to keep in touch. Smith, for his part, went off and together with Goodier created a show that plugged the gaps between daytime and Peel. It was Peel himself who'd been occupying the evening slot for a time. But when he moved to weekends, *The Evening Session* started in the first week of October 1990.

"When we started, we were asked to do a show which was magazine-y – a lot of topical speech content," Goodier revealed a year after the show went on air. "We were supposed to go for lots of meetings to tell them what we were doing, and we didn't go to one."

What they were doing was working on the music content of the new programme. Plus Goodier still had a 'day job', which contributed to the show's perception problem. People were a little suspicious of him.

"Yeah, very much, because of where I'd come from... I used to do *The Weekend Breakfast Show*. But Radio 1 asked me to do this show because they knew I'd done something similar before. I don't blame people for being suspicious. I'd probably be the same myself, but we just got our heads down and did it.

"When we first started, I think people just saw this show as the one that had taken over from John Peel so they expected just someone else playing the same records so we had to... we sat down and thought we want to play bands which aren't getting played anywhere else.

"And we reckoned at the time EMF and Gary Clail weren't. Carter weren't. And that was the area that, with a bit of help, these bands might break through from. Peel's still doing a good job, but his show is uncompromising and I guess our show is the compromise between what your average pop music listener will take and what Peel will do."

I kept in touch with Jeff, off and on, while I was at *NME*. But even so I was a little surprised when he phoned me at the paper and asked if I wanted to come in and play some records one night. The segment featured four tunes (including tracks by indie hopefuls World Of Twist and Bleach) with myself and Mark discussing the future of pop.

The *Session* itself went from strength to strength. It covered much of the same ground that we did at *NME* and, like the Peel show, featured sessions recorded at the BBC's Maida Vale studios. Among the bands booked by Smith and Goodier were Nirvana in November 1991, Suede early in 1992, and the two (aforementioned) sessions in relatively quick succession from Blur in 1992 and then again in 1993.

By the time I left the *NME*, the guest appearance had led to a regular monthly slot reviewing the week's music papers. Then they upped the ante. Mark Goodier was going to be away from the show for four weeks and instead of bringing in another Radio 1 jock to deputise, Jeff and Mark invited four young whippersnappers to take a week each.

The fantastic four were Richard Easter (who worked on the Steve Wright show), Claire Sturgess (one of Simon Bates' backroom staff), Jo Whiley (music researcher for *The Word*) and Steve Lamacq (reformed pinball addict and part-time reviews editor at *Select*). All I had to do was record a reasonable demo to convince them that I could string two sentences together and play the right jingle at the right time. It was the scariest 15 minutes of my life. At Q102 the equipment numbered two decks, a cassette player and six faders. The Radio 1 desk, as it's known, had about 100 faders and 60 switches. It was like swapping the control panel of a Mini Cooper for flying Concorde.

Eight minutes into the recording I pressed a start button, and the desk went dead.

Several thoughts flashed through my mind, but "Oh shit" was the main one. "I seem to have broken Radio 1." In the next-door studio Simon Bates, who had been live on air, was rushing around turning pink, while a couple of fraught-looking producers gesticulated at the technical staff behind the glass partition. A minute later Bates was in my studio. "Have you got power in here, love?"

"Sorry. I, erm, well, no, to be honest I think I've…"

Bates tore back out of the studio just as an engineer wandered in through the other door. "Power failure," she mumbled. "You might as well go home," she added, plodding back to the corridor.

So that was that.

They gave me the first of the four guest weeks, and on the Monday Jeff talked me through the running order. To make sure that I didn't cock it up too badly, the plan was to pre-record the first 12 minutes of the first show, so that at least the start of the programme would be OK if nothing else.

Unfortunately, ten minutes before going on air, the all-powerful controller of Radio 1, Johnny Beerling, arrived in the studio to say hello and wish me luck. "It's part of our job to encourage and nurture new talent," he went on, as the minutes ticked away. Jeff was about to ditch the tape – but Beerling departed with two minutes to spare.

After those initial weeks, Radio 1 employed Claire Sturgess to present a rock show. A few weeks later Jo and I were invited back for a fortnight each. Then they teamed us up together for a further nine-week stint. By this point, Beerling had departed and a new controller, Matthew Bannister, had arrived as the network's boss. It was soon clear that he was ready to ring the changes, and three years into the new decade, he was about to start dragging Radio 1 – belatedly – into the nineties.

As the old-school DJs either resigned or were released, the speculation about a new daytime line-up increased. The tabloids were tipping Steve Wright for *The Breakfast Show*, and, just to make Jo and I feel a little more insecure, had Nicky Campbell down to take over the evening slot. With three weeks of our dep left, we got the call. Could we go and meet Matthew?

Jo and I have talked about this since, but the way I remember it, Matthew talked a little about his plans to improve the station, while we sat like schoolchildren in the headmaster's office, averting our gaze and staring at our DMs. "So," Matthew continued. "I'd just like to say thanks very much for everything you've done..."

This was it – the SACK! A brilliant career as Somebody Like John Peel cut short, even before it had started.

"... and we'd like you to carry on, if that's alright with you."

CHRIST! DID HE JUST SAY WHAT I THINK HE JUST SAID?

"If you'd like to go and see Andy Parfitt, he'll talk through the details of your contract."

There was another bit about keeping the news secret, and then we backed out of the room, issuing a stream of thank yous. Honestly, if we'd have had caps to doff, we'd have been doffing for Britain. I'm surprised I didn't bow and call Matthew 'Your Majesty'. We made it to the lift, before exploding and hugging each other.

It's odd looking back at this now. Matthew took quite a risk with us. I mean, we'd both had some radio experience (Jo had had a spell at Radio 5 and there was my pirate show). But he could have gone for an easier, more reliable bet. One of the favourites, maybe, instead of an each-way punt.

Because I'll own up, when Jo Whiley and I first broadcast *The Evening Session* together we'd met twice, possibly three times – and had one hour's rehearsal.

Actually, that's not exactly true. We did have an hour's rehearsal time booked in a studio. But how do you rehearse a radio programme? I mean, we gave it a go. We played a few records and made up a few links, and then after 20 minutes we realised it wasn't working, so we gave up and went for a coffee.

Our two main weapons during our nine-week trial period were, put simply, adrenalin and fear. Mostly it was fear. We had this 'What if?' philosophy at the time. What if I fluff my lines? What if I press the wrong button? What if I forget what I'm saying halfway through a link? What if I say something so utterly stupid that I am booed out of the building?

The fear carried us through, and when the fear and adrenalin weren't enough we employed the ancient skills of busking and winging it. Jeff Smith, our first producer, helped. Having been there at the start of the *Sesh*, he knew how he wanted the programme to sound (pacey, informative, friendly, credible) and how to make it appear deceptively slick. The fact that, after Mark Goodier's departure, the show was now being presented by these two herberts who had nothing more than nerves and enthusiasm on their side didn't deter him at all. We were like kids at his DJ school.

"And today, class, here's how to segue a record properly."

Much of the way I still do radio today is based on tips I picked up from Jeff in the first two months at Radio 1. But even he couldn't save us from our own lapses of concentration. On our first outside broadcast – seven weeks into the trial run – we did a series of shows from the In The City seminar in Manchester. The mixing desk was set up in a hotel conference suite... and, in my defence, the equipment was completely different to what we used back in London. But 20 minutes into the first programme I stopped the CD that was playing on air.

If there is such a thing as a HUGE silence, then there was a huge silence.

Jeff, jumping up from his seat, looked like he was about to be run over by a truck.

Not sure what to do next, I opened the mic and lied for Britain.

"Well, we've got a wiring problem with the studio here, which means one of the CD players has broken down. But never mind. Here's another tune."

So we got by, and fluffed a few links, and helped disguise each other's moments of panic. As it turned out, though, we needn't have worried that much about our early failings. Shortly after we'd been handed the show full-time we received a letter from a listener that said: "Dear Jo and Steve. Love the show. Particularly the mistakes. They're funny. Do you rehearse them?"

We really couldn't have been in a better place at a better time. Just a couple of months after being employed to host *The Evening Session* full-time, we started 1994 with the debut session from a band just signed to Creation records called... Oasis. For the second time in my life I'd accidentally become caught up in The Bigger Scheme Of Things: a revolution in both music and media.

Pop was changing, Radio 1 was changing. The playlist was also starting to improve, along with the emergence of Britpop and club anthems, both inside and outside the chart. It was hard to recognise the place from a year earlier when I'd first appeared on *The Evening Session*.

Not only did I catch a whiff of DLT's aftershave on my first visit, but while I was sitting in reception waiting to be allowed up to the studio, the familiar sight of Simon Bates hove into view through the front door. Bates walked up to the reception desk and, proffering a carrier bag, said to the man stationed there: "Alright to leave this here with you? I'll pick it up in the morning. I'm always first in."

Unfortunately, the security man must have been new, or short-sighted, because as Bates dropped the bag and turned on his heels, he called after him. "Wait a minute. What's your name?"

Bates: "I'm BATES."

Security man: "And your first name?"

All the DJs who were still there when Jo and I joined scared me witless, although many of them were very kind to us. Steve Wright used to beckon us into the studio for a chat and would share his cigarillos with us; Simon Mayo was evidently a nice chap; and there was Goodier, of course. But it took me months to get up the bottle to speak to John Peel.

And there we were, if not at the centre of it, at least close by. I can't pretend we weren't still insecure about our position (after all, we'd only been offered a year-long contract, and then, as far as I could see in my darker moments, it was straight back out on the street). But at least we had a foot in the door.

CHAPTER 17

No More Heroes

Annoying things bands do:

- They release the wrong singles from albums.
- They 'mature'.
- They split up just before you're about to see them play live.
- They split up just after you've bought the album and the T-shirt.
- They never play your favourite song live (and if they do, they announce: "This is the last time we're ever going to do this one").
- They go through pointless image changes.
- They turn round and tell you that their last album was rubbish – having spent the previous three years telling you how great it was.
- Your favourite member of the band quits.
- They add a needless keyboard player.
- They disappear for 18 months to write and record, just when you need them most.

- They moan about money.

- They tour with all the wrong bands.

- They cover rock classics (badly).

- They dream up endless new ways to hurt and humiliate you.

How do they manage to do all this? And, more to the point, why do we let them get away with it? I've got two explanations for this. One is that, as pop fans, we suffer from misplaced loyalty. The second is that the older and apparently wiser folk among us have simply become resigned to the fact that bands cock it up. However great they seem when they start, and however much they appear to say about your life – and wrap you up warm against the cruel outside world – they will, with a sad and stunning inevitably, let you down in the end.

My problem is that I still fall for it. I know bands are fallible but I still pray for a group – or a DJ, or a musical scene – that is superhuman and untouchable.

Mind you, I'm not as bad as I used to be. I've progressed past the stage where I carried on buying singles by bands long after I knew they'd lost the plot (why else are there so many unplayed and unplayable Stranglers' singles lurking in a box in the cupboard?). I really don't know what I was thinking of. Did I expect them to repay my faith by suddenly doing a career U-turn and returning to their old selves? Or was I simply in a state of denial? (Note: The last Stranglers' album was actually very good, but I'm not sure if that is enough of an olive branch to make me forget the past.)

There are two problems when bands go bad. Not only do you have to admit it to yourself, you then have to decide whether to go public and admit it to other people. Friends, enemies even. Non-believers. Oh God, the shame. It's easy to get angry or upset with a record by a band you don't care that much about (in fact, it's quite therapeutic). But getting angry and upset with your favourite band is completely different. They have thrown you to the lions. HOW COULD THEY DO THIS TO US?

It's a shocking state of affairs but it took me until my twenties to have the strength to start admitting that the groups I liked could get it wrong. I'm not sure if there was one group who forced this admission out of me, but it's more likely it was a gradual process (like slowly realising that your suspicions about the existence of Father Christmas had been true all along).

Now I go through life as an optimistic pessimist. My latest band of the moment will evolve into the best group in the world. And if they don't, well, I'll deal with it. I have armed myself with excuses now for why bands go wrong (bad management, bad record label, bad timing – it's nearly always someone else's fault). So that's OK. We won't get fooled again.

But the scars are still there, though. And none of them are deeper than when bands I've fallen in love with have gone and split up. I remember the first time it happened. Graham Diss told me at school one day that The Lurkers were no more. Now, the news wasn't that much of a shock. There'd been no sign of the band for months and their last single, 'New Guitars In Town', had peaked at number 72 in the chart. So it wasn't such a big surprise. I think what hurt was that they hadn't had the decency to tell me. Graham Diss knew. He'd written a letter to their label, Beggars Banquet, asking for news and freebies and they'd sent him a letter saying "The Lurkers are no more, but here's some badges to make up for it." Badges!

And there was I, a fully paid-up member of The Lurkers' Flan Cub – their little joke (cringe) – and I didn't know. This was as bad as finding your girlfriend in the arms of another. Not only had The Lurkers, the object of my infatuation, split up, but they'd been unfaithful in the process.

And yet, when they came crawling back, reforming first in 1980 and then in 1988, I forgave them both times. The first time they had a new singer; the second time they were led by original bassist Arturo Bassick, who softened the blow by phoning me at the *NME*, out of the blue, and asking if it was true that I'd been a long-standing fan of the group. Well, yes actually. OK, so can you write the sleeve notes for the new live album?

As part of this deal I made them come and meet me in the *NME* pub, much to the amusement of the rest of the staff (the idea that the young gun A&R scout was entertaining a bunch of old punk rockers was all too much for them). But for me, it was like an apology. They turned up and bought drinks and told stories about the old days. They even admitted that the second album sounded wet, and quite rightly blamed the American producer for it. And I finally put the incident with the badges behind me. More recently, three of the original members of the band came into 6 Music to celebrate the fortieth anniversary of their debut single, 'Shadow'.

But I can still sympathise with anyone who's gone through a similar experience. For instance, the band Symposium broke up just after I started writing this book in 2000, and within days of our announcing the split on air, I was inundated with letters and emails from upset fans.

Each one wept with the same phrases: 'How could they do this?' and 'Tell me it's not true.' Well, I'm sorry, but it *is* true. It's harsh and it hurts, but time is a great healer and you'll get over them.

What does all this say about our relationship with bands – particularly in our teens? Does it say that some of us are too obsessed for our own good? Or does it say that bands are rubbish? That's right. Pop groups are rubbish.

For once, take note of the Gallaghers, and please, PLEASE, don't put your life in the hands of a rock'n'roll band.

CHAPTER 18

Shakermaker

On the Thursday night of Radio 1's Sound City festival in Glasgow, Danbert Nobacon of anarcho-punk pop band Chumbawamba walked naked through the bar of the Forte Crest Hotel. I guess it was around 2 a.m. He must have marched past about 50 late-night drinkers (made up of other bands, managers, press officers, roadies and journalists), and do you know what happened? None of them batted an eyelid.

Now I've thought about this a lot over the years, and the first assumption I come to is that, to put it bluntly, no one really cared about a naked member of Chumbawamba (possibly because the band were always considered a little eccentric by the rest of the rock fraternity). But being a theorist, there's an alternative explanation that I'd much rather believe. I'd like to think that this was the week that rock music was about to change forever and that the man to change it wasn't, sadly, going to be Danbert Nobacon.

One group who had set the wheels of change turning had already been and gone – in fact, they'd left Glasgow a few hours earlier. The other man responsible for changing the course of rock was thousands of miles away in America. Together, however, they were the ones about to make the week's headlines. Enter Oasis, exit Nirvana.

*

It was at the small but famous Glasgow haunt King Tut's – situated just around the corner from the Forte Crest – that Creation records boss Alan McGee saw the nascent Oasis for the first time, supporting future labelmates 18 Wheeler. And it was back to Glasgow that the band came for their first live appearance on Radio 1 and their first major interview for *NME*.

This was the week when everything fell into place for Oasis; when you knew that they were really going places. I'm sure in their own heads they were practically superstars already, but if the rest of the media needed any convincing then here was the proof. One guerrilla raid on Glasgow, one gig and one amazing interview in the course of a few hours set them up for the rest of 1994. Their timing was immaculate.

Having been serviced with a single-track promo of 'Columbia' at Radio 1, the *Session* producer Christine Boar leapt on the 12-inch and booked a session by the band at our Maida Vale studios. It was recorded just before Christmas 1993 and broadcast in the first week of January 1994 – that key time when pundits and fans alike are looking for new bands to champion for the year ahead. In fact, not only did the session run, but 'Columbia' made the Radio 1 playlist, guaranteeing it coverage throughout the day.

It didn't take a massive leap of faith to follow up the station's support by booking them for Sound City – then Radio 1's annual live music festival. Sound City evolved a good deal over the years, but in 1994 it was still in its infancy. Previous Sound City events in Norwich and Sheffield had featured some bizarre and eclectic choices of bands. And 1994 wasn't much different (M People, Inspiral Carpets, Therapy?, Urban Species).

For Jo and me, Sound City was a completely new challenge. Having started to cope with the idea of broadcasting on national radio, we were now faced with the prospect of introducing bands on stage, live on air. Now, this may not seem like the most frightening prospect in the world – and I'd certainly rather compere a gig than sit in a dentist's chair for an hour – but I've never found it that easy either. You have a producer talking to you through an earpiece; you have a crowd in front of you; and you have the devil on your shoulder trying to make you slip up and say the F word.

On top of that, I'm among the people who believe that if you're not in the band, then what are you doing on stage? We've all seen roadies who love running onto the stage and finding problems to deal with (the drum mic is an inch too far to the left or there's a speck of water by the singer's foot which needs mopping up in case they slip on it). That's OK. I can forgive them. But anyone else is just in the way.

And this time it was me. If you've ever been to one of our live radio gigs, you might notice that I try to get on and off a stage as quickly as possible. I don't mean to be rude, but I don't want to outstay my welcome either. In Glasgow, there was a delay before Inspiral Carpets came on and I had to hang around as people threw empty cigarette packets at me. Inspirals' keyboard player Clint Boon very kindly defused the situation by starting up a chant of "You thin bastard! You thin bastard!" That did the trick.

I was incredibly lucky as well because I had some friendly faces from the *NME* hanging out in Glasgow through the week. And that helped with the nerves. Williams was there, photographer Roger Sargeant, Keith Cameron, and John Harris, who was the man with the plan. He was there to interview Oasis.

NME had first interviewed them just a few weeks earlier, for the paper's On section, but in the same way that the Mondays had made the press an occupied zone in 1989, Oasis were already a band who couldn't keep out of the headlines. Between the last interview and this one they'd played an astonishing gig at the tiny Water Rats venue in London. And they'd been refused entry to Holland because of their drunken behaviour on the cross-channel ferry.

It was this incident which had created a rift between the Gallagher brothers, exposed to great effect by the *NME* piece. It was such a charged confrontation that highlights even turned up later on a single called 'Wibbling Rivalry'. On it you hear the tension twixt the brothers, with Harris in the middle refereeing. Every time he thinks he's got them to return to their corners, they come back out fighting.

It was riveting.

*

Oasis announced their overdue arrival in the same week that Nirvana's Kurt Cobain made his tragic exit. Two days after the Oasis radio appearance, and the morning after the Nobacon No Clothes incident, news began seeping through from the States that Cobain had committed suicide at his home in Seattle. To all intents and purposes, the grunge movement as an energetic, creative force died with him.

The problem with bands like Nirvana is that they bring with them a handful of groups who all sell a few records but are, in all honesty, worthy runners-up. They are good team players but they're not captains. They're not big or strong enough to shoulder a movement, at least not without the movement reinventing itself. (Grunge, having licked its wounds, later made something of a comeback with the likes of Smashing Pumpkins, not to mention the Foo Fighters, who eventually transcended grunge to become simply a Bloody Huge Rock Band – much, I imagine, to Dave Grohl's delight, having once said at a gig that "Grunge can never die, because grunge was never born.")

Cobain's suicide sent a shiver through the industry. We knew all the stories. Kurt and drugs, the tough love therapy, the cancelled gigs, his unhappiness with the rock-star status he'd acquired. But we had never imagined life without him.

As people gathered in the foyer of the hotel, ready to leave for home, the news started to filter round the room (late risers had seen it on TV or heard the first reports on the radio). Everyone looked stunned, simply unable to cope with the bad news and a hangover at the same time. Kurt was gone. What the hell happens now?

CHAPTER 19

Common People

Looking back, it's obvious that Britain had begun to lust after a music scene all its own, but explaining how it finally fell into place is another, much trickier, matter.

Yes, a lot of what was happening in the UK from 1991 onwards was a reaction to grunge. But not everything that Britain touted as the Next Big Thing proved successful. And there were several false starts before Oasis and co. strode forth into the chart in 1994.

The first difficulty with Britpop is picking a start point. But, for the sake of argument, let's stick a pin into the spring of 1993. Suede had already arrived – dubbed the Best New Band In Britain by *Melody Maker* in 1992 – and Blur's rehabilitation into a cred-pop band had begun as well. In April, *Select* magazine ran with the first Britpop-style cover, featuring Suede's Brett Anderson on the cover, dressed in black leather and superimposed on a Union Jack. The cover line was "Yanks Go Home! Suede, St Etienne, Denim, Pulp, The Auteurs And The Battle For Britain".

As a concept piece it spoke volumes about the changes in critical opinion at the time. Inside it ranted: "We don't want your plaid! We want crimplene, glamour, wit and irony."

What's the old adage? 'Be careful what you wish for, some of it might come true'? Luckily it wasn't the bit about crimplene.

Unwittingly, though, *Select* had hit on something here, which is the dress up/dress down phenomenon that you can trace right back to the start of rock'n'roll. If one scene prides itself on looking smart, the next will want to be scruffy. And if the two ever met? Well, you got running battles on Brighton beach.

I've watched this since the seventies. For glam rock you dressed up and had long hair; for punk you dressed down and went short and spiky. After the perceived scruffiness of punk came the suits of the mod revival and the 2-tone ska bands, not to mention the walking flower arrangements of the new romantic movement. In the eighties there was the post-rocker look of the Midlands grebo bands, followed by the smarter, hipper, new casual baggy style of the Madchester scene. Post-baggy you had grunge... and after the plaid fad of grunge came the first wave of Britpop.

A month after the 'Yanks Go Home' cover, Suede's debut album arrived, which I found myself reviewing in my new role as the magazine's reviews editor (in response, their PR company enclosed four cans of cider with the review copy of the record). We gave the album four out of five – not for the free cider but because, at the time, it was a genuinely refreshing record. There were elements of David Bowie, yes, but I think I also compared it to the first Adam & The Ants album mixed with the plotlines of various Dennis Potter plays. Whichever way you called it, though, it was a decidedly English-sounding first outing. So much so that Brett Anderson told *The Evening Session* that when Suede played one of their first gigs in Scotland, they were petrified for their lives.

"This really tall punk with a Mohican stood at the front of the gig all night, and between songs pointed at us and shouted: 'You effete southern wankers.'"

In the same year Blur released their second album, *Modern Life Is Rubbish*, complete with a series of press shots which had captions like 'British Image Number 2'. In the photos, the previously bowl-haired pretty boys had swapped their pop image for Fred Perrys, DMs and cheap suits. Was there a theme here?

If there was, then there wasn't any time for it to solidify. Instead, in an attempt to outgun its punky American counterparts, the

NME came up with the short, sharp shock of the New Wave Of New Wave.

If anything reveals how desperate everyone was for a new British guitar movement, then it must have been the NWONW. (Even the concept of selling a whole new scene based on two or three bands is very British. You didn't find it anywhere else in the world's media. But then the rest of the world was bereft of weekly papers and the music scene didn't move as quickly as it did in Britain.)

The NWONW – a title poached from the short-lived late seventies/early eighties British rock scene dubbed the New Wave Of British Heavy Metal – was a frantic, speed-fuelled attempt to launch a handful of bands at the chart and reclaim the guitar baton from America. Come to think of it, 'baton' makes it sound like a race. Maybe a better sporting analogy would be the Ryder Cup or the Ashes. Instead of playing the Aussies at cricket we could play America at rock genres.

The groups involved with NWONW weren't all bad. We even got in there early and played a demo by one of them, S*M*A*S*H, on *The Evening Session* to a general thumbs up all round. But in the end I think their uncompromising attitude and lack of subtlety undermined them. Maybe S*M*A*S*H were even too overtly political for the time (their best single, 'I Want To Kill Somebody', included a hitlist of Tory MPs).

As well as S*M*A*S*H, there was These Animal Men, and Elastica got lumped in there too. But the NWONW wasn't a strong enough or broad enough platform for all the bands that started to emerge through 1994. At *The Evening Session* we played a white-label seven-inch from Backbeat Records by some new group called Supergrass who all my mates were raving about. And for a time, it felt like each week brought a promising new debut record. There was Sleeper, Ash, Echobelly and Gene, whose limited-edition first single even made the Radio 1 playlist.

The response from the listeners was terrific. On the crest of the new wave, Radio 1 decamped to the movement's spiritual home on the south coast for a week of *Evening Session* shows called 'Brighton Rocks'. I have several poignant memories of this week, the most ridiculous being sent out by Radio 1 to compile a five-minute feature on the pubs of Brighton and arriving in the final one to find Bob Grover, singer with original new wave group The Piranhas, hunched in a corner over a lunchtime pint.

It was a curious week of gigs. The Fugees flew in especially from America to play (supporting Transglobal Underground). The Prodigy also appeared; as did Brit-rap acts Kaliphz and Honky. But the rest of the live bands were the ones that had crashed ashore on the new wave – some of whom would later become the sandcastles of Britpop. Elastica led the way, but during the week there were also sets by Shed 7, Sleeper, Gene, Echobelly, These Animal Men and Lush.

Oh, it rained every day. It really did.

To my knowledge, no one really coined the term Britpop until around the start of 1995. By then, with all the pieces laid out in a jumble on the floor, Britpop started to fit together like a jigsaw. If you take Blur and Suede as the corners (they're the easy bits to start with), then Elastica fitted in between them. Having slotted Justine and co. in, then many of the bands who followed snapped into place quite quickly. Supergrass's 'Caught By The Fuzz' had a similar feel to Elastica's debut 'Stutter'. Then there was Ash, who toured with Elastica, and the 60ft Dolls, who garnered some of their early attention through their links with old friend and Elastica guitarist Donna Matthews. Other groups fitted together because of other factors behind the scenes. Either the same people signed them, or the same press officer plugged them.

Even the difficult bits – those that, when we started, didn't seem to fit anywhere – all of a sudden fell into place. There was Radiohead (who in jigsaw terms were a difficult piece of sky). And there were the oddly shaped pieces that you pick up and put down and come back to later. The misshapes. Which is why the last important piece to go in was Pulp.

Everyone will have their own defining Britpop moments. But for what it's worth, these are mine:

- The Parklife tour.

- Pulp going to number two in the charts with 'Common People'.

- 'Country House' versus 'Roll With It'.

Of these, if I had to pick one point in time when you knew the world had gone (Britpop) mad, then it was the release of 'Common People'. Interested parties within the music industry had already become aware of the buzz surrounding the track, long before it hit the shops. It had been promoted to alternative clubs some weeks ahead of its release, to a surprisingly good reaction. (Indie clubs are notoriously conservative when it comes to new music, but 'Common People', which had already been played to death on Radio 1, was an exception.)

The day before the chart was unveiled I was guest DJ at Nottingham Rock City, and Mike, the resident DJ, was frothing with excitement over the news of its possible chart position: "It's number two midweek… Number two!" Number two was a big deal. Number two was almost unbelievable. Number two was notice that the lunatics had taken over the asylum.

Here was the band who had spent years selling 22 copies of each record they'd released finally selling 80,000 in ONE WEEK. And that singer, who we'd always said was going to be a star, now really was GOING TO BE A STAR.

But there was more to it than even that, because Britpop – a scene that thrived on the best and worst English excesses – had succeeded in producing one of Britain's favourite and most romantic phenomena: the victorious underdog.

Pulp were a band who had succeeded against the odds. If you look at the rest of the Britpop groups, including Oasis and Elastica, they'd had a relatively straightforward career. Sure, Oasis had put in the graft, rehearsing day in, day out at the Manchester Boardwalk, and Suede – another of Pulp's peers – had lived off tins of cold baked beans in various damp Camden flats before their break had come. But Pulp had been trying to crack it for years.

My introduction to them came via Dave Bedford at Fire Records who gave me a copy of one of their old singles, 'Little Girl With

Blue Eyes', just as the group were about to re-emerge onto the London circuit in 1991. A few weeks later came their new single, 'My Legendary Girlfriend' – an *NME* single of the week – and then a few of us trooped out to West London to see them play at a venue called Subterania. Subterania was a bastard to get to, and it seemed like every indie gig there was barely half full, but the record was good enough to warrant a live review so I bowled up, not sure what to expect, and then Alvin Stardust walked on stage. Or at least it was someone who posed a little like Alvin Stardust, but it couldn't have been Alvin Stardust because he had brown cords and glasses on.

"Pulp provide another lucid, sometimes eccentric view of music," I scribbled away in the review of the gig. "Outfront, singer/satirist Jarvis Cocker sashays around the stage, part Elvis Presley, part John Travolta.

"'It's a bit like playing on somebody's fireplace here,' says Cocker. 'I don't know if you can see, but it's all tiled around the stage. You could put a couple of horse brasses up on the walls, give it a bit of atmosphere. Until then, here's another song.'

"The disco-boogie-angst of 'Countdown', the next single in June, is followed by the climactic current 45 'My Legendary Girlfriend' – complete with cock-up in the middle. It's very grand, but it's top entertainment."

I remember the cock-up. I saw Pulp about three times around this point and every night Nick Banks would launch his drums into the final part of the song eight bars too early – and every time he did it, Cocker turned round, shook his head and stared at him. Could have been part of the act, for all I know.

'My Legendary Girlfriend' earned them a lot of praise in the press and sold in the region of 1,500 copies, but Pulp's career still managed to hit the skids again. There was a falling-out with the record label, problems with management and all kinds of drama until they found their way. But Pulp were so endearing that however badly they were doing, someone always seemed to turn up who had faith in them.

I'm not sure what to attribute this to. Was it Jarvis's charisma? Pulp's music? Or was it just that they all thought this band deserved a break? Whatever, Pulp secured the services of one of London's leading music PR companies (who were so convinced of the band's future that they did their publicity for free). And then they met Geoff Travis from Rough Trade. Travis – of whom more later in this book – helped re-energise both Cocker and Pulp's prospects of fame.

The band signed to Island Records and recorded *His 'N' Hers*. And in April 1994 they had their first Top 40 hit with 'Do You Remember The First Time?'. With bands like Suede and Blur around, Pulp no longer seemed to be as musically out on a limb as they previously had been (prior to their association with Britpop, the only band that had come into their orbit was a spangly, futuristic group called World Of Twist who'd had a couple of minor hits at the start of the nineties).

Not only that, but Jarvis was running up the star ladder, two rungs at a time. As we cheered him on, he appeared first on BBC TV's *Pop Quiz*, where he shocked everyone with his extraordinary knowledge of both credible and cheesy pop trivia. Then, with Pulp having been to America and narrowly lost the Mercury Music Prize to M People, he hosted *Top Of The Pops* and famously introduced the number one band of the week with the words: "Take That ARE Top Of The Pops." From that show onwards, every presenter was told to finish the show with the same phrase.

His 'N' Hers had made it into the Top 10 of the album chart, and Pulp went about their business working on a follow-up. The starting point was 'Common People'. Stop me if you've heard this one before, but the story goes like this. Having sold some records in the Notting Hill branch of Record and Tape Exchange, Cocker immediately reinvested the money in an old Casio keyboard.

A few days later, fiddling around with the Casio at rehearsal, he played a tune to guitarist Steve Mackey. "After we both stopped laughing," Jarvis told me once, "he said it sounded like 'Fanfare For The Common Man'. And that's where I got the idea for the words from." They first recorded 'Common People' for a John Peel session in the autumn of 1994 and then went in to the studio where they spent a week recording it for release.

As they came to the mixing stage, however, Jarvis decided the track wasn't sounding right. There was something missing. The problem was that it didn't sound chuggy enough. Unable to conjure up the right explanation, he went to his record collection and found the chuggiest record he could find. He sat producer Chris Thomas down and played him... 'Mr Blue Sky' by Electric Light Orchestra.

Can you imagine how bewildered Thomas must have been? Here's a man who's worked with the Sex Pistols, The Pretenders and some of the biggest names in rock being told that the track they've sweated over for days on end should sound more like the invention of ELO – an opera-obsessed seventies rock orchestra led by Jeff Lynne, a man held together by a beard and dark glasses.

Thomas did the trick, though, and Jarvis added some acoustic guitar, and bingo. Pulp had 'Common People' in the bag.

The next problem was persuading Island Records that they should release it straight away. The label was wary of putting out a single without the entire new album being finished and ready to go. But Cocker was convinced that at last – after years of hanging around – Pulp were finally in the right place at the right time. Blur and Oasis had just had huge hits. The record-buying masses were ready. Island concurred and Pulp went to number two.

"We used to have a rivalry going between Food Records and Savage and Best [Pulp's PR company]," Andy Ross from Food told me a while later. "You could see one of the windows of their office from ours, and we used to stick up midweek chart positions of our bands versus theirs.

"When 'Common People' came out, I got a fax with Pulp's midweek on it and rang them up to congratulate them. I said, '21, that's really good.' I didn't realise the one was really an exclamation mark."

CHAPTER 20

Four Skinny Indie Kids

Just as the world of high finance has a base in the Square Mile of the City of London, Britpop developed its own centre for movers and shakers. Except the high-powered execs and bright young things of pop weren't in the East London commuter zone, they were all in Camden.

The centre of the pop economy was in a square mile around Camden Town Tube station, with the Good Mixer to the west, Dingwalls and the Monarch to the north, the Falcon to the east and the Camden Palace with its Tuesday night Feet First Club to the south.

Camden was the big noise. It had been through sporadic periods of notoriety before, but nothing like this. The invasion of bands and fans and tourists that took place through the mid- to late nineties was so huge that Britpop even drove some of the Camden old guard out of the borough altogether.

Among the groups to flee were Gallon Drunk – a stylish band of bluesmen who, ironically, were the group who had first made the Good Mixer semi-famous in 1992 when they did all their interviews there. But that's jumping ahead of the game. Camden's first flirtation with fame in the nineties was centred more to the south-east, where Jeff Barrett was promoting bands at the Falcon. The Falcon became one of the two breeding ground venues which played host to a handful of infectiously noisy local groups including Silverfish and Th' Faith Healers. If anything, these bands were British grunge before there was even American grunge (so you can imagine the complaints from the neighbours). Together they were shouty and hairy and their followers used to do a strange lunging sort of dance, which involved tipping themselves backwards and forwards from the waist in a bastardisation of headbanging.

In fact, it was at the Falcon that these bands got their nickname. One night watching Silverfish, I suggested that the dance was 'less Lambeth Walk, more Camden Lurch'. BINGO. Having had features on both the Healers and Silverfish turned down at *NME*, we went back in with news of the new Camden lurch scene and within minutes had been commissioned to write a two-page spread about it. Never mind that lurch was really only three or four bands (if you included Milk and Sun Carriage), it was a good way of squeezing Camden and its underground culture into the paper. Sadly, they didn't use the suggested headline 'The Chords Of The New Lurch'.

The other fan-based venue at the time was the Hampstead White Horse, which had a series of nights running called the Sausage Machine. It was the Sausage Machine which finally spawned a new record label called Too Pure, which signed Th' Faith Healers and later P. J. Harvey and Stereolab. Together with the nascent Wiiija label (based in West London, but spiritually at home in Camden), there was a feeling that something was happening here. Wiiija had Silverfish and then signed Therapy? from Northern Ireland and the noise-mongering continued.

Meanwhile, back in Inverness Street, Gallon Drunk released a gloriously embittered single called 'Some Fools Mess' and we did the follow-up *NME* feature in the Good Mixer. I couldn't believe the place. The feature even started with the line "Somewhere in Camden there is a pub that time forgot..." There was an old seven-inch jukebox on the wall, two old men in the corner, and Gallon Drunk in their vintage suits playing pool. It was like stepping back in time 20 years.

But that was the appeal of the Mixer. Not only did it seem like the most eccentric pub in London, you could always get a seat, and it had a good jukebox. They were the same things that appealed to the staff of Food Records, who moved in round the corner in 1992, and then the PR firm Savage and Best (whose clientele included Suede, Pulp and the fledgling Elastica), who arrived next door to Food in 1993. Both firms were to become synonymous with Britpop; both drank in the Mixer. In fact, both used the Mixer for business.

Savage and Best used to take their bands there to be interviewed, while Food were in another corner chatting up potential new signings. Embarrassingly, I barged in on a Food Records A&R meeting once by mistake to hear Dave Balfe grilling a group called Three And A Half Minutes about their manifesto for making it.

As the Mixer's notoriety spread among journalists and bands, the pub started being namechecked in the music paper gossip columns. Through 1993 and 1994, the clientele began to change. Not only did the numbers grow, but the type of customer started to change too. Out went the drinkers who were living off the proceeds of their last trip to Record and Tape Exchange. In came the day trippers with their HMV carrier bags who wanted to finish off their shopping spree with a couple of hours of celebrity-spotting.

The Square Mile – and the Mixer in particular – was happy to oblige. Blur, Elastica, Pulp and even Morrissey drank in the Mixer in 1994, while Noel Gallagher moved in to a flat in the area in 1995. The Mixer became the trading floor, the home of the hustlers – it was the FTSE Index of Britpop (Blur up four, The Bluetones up two, Thurman down six). To add to the packed crowds doing business in the Mixer, the Dublin Castle, around the corner in Camden Parkway, became the venue of choice for the A&R scouts of the day.

Camden venues went in and out of fashion, not because of the decor or the drinks they served, but because of who was booking the gigs. By 1995 a guy called Chris Myhill, previously a booker at the Kentish Town Bull and Gate and a man with a good ear for a new band, had taken charge of some of the gigs. And the Castle, which had spent years in the doldrums having once been home to the band Madness, once again became a good hunting ground for talent.

Monday nights in particular were an A&R hot ticket. Just like the days of Dingwalls Panic Station, I used to leave work and head straight up there (prior to the start of my old *Lamacq Live* show, *The Evening Session* used to finish at 8.30 p.m. so I used to arrive halfway through the first band). Along with Myhill, the Monday Club Spangle nights were organised by Simon Williams and Nude Records A&R man David Laurie. Of the bands they booked, several went on to get record deals or end up on the *Sesh*.

I spent a lot of these Monday nights trying to come up with a collective noun for A&R scouts. Well, when you're stuck in a corner waiting to see the next band, there's not much else to do. But there they'd be, gangs of A&R staff turning up en masse, trying to find the new Blur or the new Oasis. They hunt in packs, you know (as brilliantly illustrated in John Niven's novel *Kill Your Friends*).

Among the gigs that attracted huge industry interest were The Bluetones and a band who, legend has it, formed in the pub just two streets away... Menswear. Menswear were the first product of the Good Mixer and the massive success of Blur's *Parklife* LP. They were hugely endearing. To me, they were the first band to form out of the audience and walk straight onto *Top Of The Pops*. But that was the mood of the Mixer and pop music in general in 1994 and 1995. It felt like anything could happen. If you could blag and hustle and charm and stand up straight for half an hour, then there was nothing you couldn't achieve.

Britpop ran on self-belief. And when the self-belief started to run thin, the cocaine kicked in to replace it. I'm not a drug user myself, because I doubt my skinny frame would be able to take such things, but coke – which was on the increase everywhere during the nineties – hit Britpop very hard. It's difficult to be specific without getting wound up in a libel action – but there are records from the later Britpop era which have all the hallmarks of being made on coke. They aren't very good. I bet they sounded great in the studio at the time though. ("LISTENTOTHISSSSSS!!!")

But anyway, one day Menswear were just five blokes who you used to see in the pub, and the next there was a drawing of them pinned to the wall of George and Niki's restaurant in Parkway

(George and Niki's was a Britpop haunt, serving roasts and fry-ups that earned it the nickname 'School Dinners'). The walls were always covered with pictures of TV celebrities. Proper famous people. Then one day there was a picture of Menswear among them. That must have sent tremors of nervous energy through the trading floor back in the Mixer.

t the Radio 1 office in Yalding House in the late nineties. No word of a lie, during an inspection by Health & Safety, an ficer stopped and took a picture of my desk as an example of poor workplace tidiness (the messiest desk 'award' having en wrestled from the equally untidy Annie Nightingale).

PRODUCTION DETAILS   (RUNNING ORDER)

ROMEO   ROMEO   ROMEO   ROMEO   ROMEO

Programme **EVENING SESSION** Presenter **J WHILEY & S LAMACQ**	SCRIPT P as B P as R	Date 18.04.94 Issue 1

Origination Prog No 94IC1108LQ0 Repeat Prog No	Tx Date Wk 16 Monday 18.04.94 Tx Date

Service R1 1900 – 2100 Waveband MW 1900 – 2100 VHF 1900 – 2100	Tx Slot 120	Stereo Y	Rot N	Music Y

Pre-rec Date	Final Tape No	Tape Dur

Producer **CHRISTINE BOAR**	Address **416 Egon House** **PABX 55275**

Programme / Contributor(s) Details	Insert No. & Rec. Date	1st TX Date (if a repeat)

THE EVENING SESSION
WITH
STEVE LAMACE (OA)
AND
JO WHILEY (OA)

IN SESSION: **ELASTICA**   4 MUS
               94IH5151LQ0   16/3/94

RPT SESSION: HONKY   6 MUS
               94IH5143LQ0   19/1/94

RPT SESSION: NIRVANA   3 MUS
               91IH5005LQ0   9/11/91

PLUS: NIRVANA TRIBUTES
INCLUDING SESSION REPEAT

STEVE'S RECORD OF THE WEEK - SLEEPER

JO'S RECORD OF THE WEEK - GENE

Issued By: Tel.Ext: Date: 18.04.94

Front page of the running order for one of our shows in the wake of Kurt Cobain's death. Turns out even some of the staff at Radio 1 couldn't spell my name correctly on some nights!

The first promo card Jo Whiley and I ever had after joining Radio 1. There was no budget, so we stuck some posters and old music papers over a wall in a basement corridor of Broadcasting House.

ne of my favourite festival photos. Being regaled backstage by the wit and wisdom of John Peel, alongside BBC engieer (and Livingstone drummer) Andy Rogers.

BLUR PARKLIFE PARTY
TUESDAY APRIL 26TH
WALTHAMSTOW GREYHOUND STADIUM
AND CHARLIE CHANS NIGHTCLUB
Chingford Road, Chingford, E4 8SJ.

8PM - GREYHOUND RACING
10PM - 1AM PARTY

THE INVITE ADMITS ONE PERSON TO CHARLIE CHANS ONLY
Entry to Walthamstow Stadium can be gained with the attached pass.
Coaches will leave EMI, 20 Manchester Square, W1. at
7PM FOR RACING
9.15PM FOR PARTY ONLY AND LEAVE CHARLIE CHANS FOR MANCHESTER SQUARE AT 1AM.
Food & drink will be supplied at Charlie Chans
RSVP Amanda Kyme - Parlophone T. 071 486 4488. Andy Ross - Food T. 071 284 2554

PARKLIFE
Parlophone

The Invite for Blur's 'Parklife' album launch at Walthamstow Greyhound Stadium.

A cheap photocopied dressing room sign, which I pilfered one night on tour. To my embarrassment, I have quite a collection of tatty dressing room signs.

Fierce Panda & Club Pointy present

CLUB PANDA
(number twelve)
featuring

COLDPLAY
"Passionate, articulate rock hoo-har with a smile sixty miles wide"

+

GREAT OUTDOORS
"They used to be the Farmers Boys. We shit you not"

+

SENSELESS PRAYER Mar 18th 1999
"Scatty, downright livid pop rumpus from Bromsgrove. You betcha!"

Bull & Gate, 389 Kentish Town Road, NW5
admission £5.00 * doors 8pm

special guest
£2.00

As well as running the Fierce Panda label, journalist Simon Williams and friends also promoted gigs at various north London venues during the nineties, including a stint at the Kentish Town Bull & Gate. The headliners went on to do OK. The Bull & Gate was shut and turned into a gastro pub.

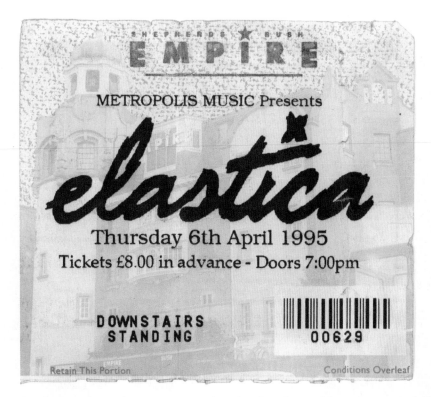

SHEPHERDS ★ BUSH
EMPIRE

METROPOLIS MUSIC Presents

elastica

Thursday 6th April 1995
Tickets £8.00 in advance - Doors 7:00pm

DOWNSTAIRS
STANDING

00629

Retain This Portion   Conditions Overleaf

I've never kept a lot of ticket stubs, much to my annoyance these days, but a few special ones have survived. This was Elastica's biggest gig to date, a wonderfully jubilant night, coming just three weeks after their debut album had gone to number one.

Taken after one of the gigs on the second Evening Session tour: myself and opening band Muse, who travelled the country in a huge, orange double-decker tour bus (not bad given that it was their first ever proper tour).

Also on the second Session tour. Broadcasting the show from the top deck of our own tour bus. We had to take out handful of seats to fit the desk in.

STEVE LAMACQ **as he is**

Job description: DJ
– Evening Session

Biggest musical influence: punk

My life in one line: going deaf
for a living

Funniest thing I've ever said:
don't worry I'll have it done by Friday

Favourite album/single: changes every week

Autograph:

One of Radio 1's promo postcards, to tie in with a new marketing campaign: Radio 1 As We Are. To cut costs, they made them double sided (flip this over and you have Jo Whiley As She Is).

The Access All Areas laminate for the first Evening Session tour. Happy days.

Put those legs away man! Another day, another tour bus: "Hello… yes, we'd like two ciders, some crisps… and the directions to the nearest curry house please."

CHAPTER 21

Street Spirit

In the bowels of the old Radio 1 building, there used to be a basement archive housing the station's old tapes and DATS and what have you. It was a marvellous place, overseen by a chap called Phil Lawton, the sort of archivist who took an indecent amount of pleasure out of looking after the Radio 1 legacy, filing away shows and sessions and one-off interviews.

Lawton was eventually released, as the BBC went on a drive to digitise its archive. (Although far be it from me to blame the digital transfer for the loss of scores of shows we did in the past. Ha!) But at the time of writing this book, Lawton was still in situ, and a terrific help, digging out dozens of old programmes and interviews. I could barely remember them then, but most of these I can't recall at all now.

But, as a snapshot of the time, like an old diary, this list gives you a little reminder of the *Session*'s main cast members through 1995.

JANUARY: Simon Williams (*NME*), Gina Morris (*Select*) and Dom Phillips (*Mixmag*) with their tips for the top. Also reports back from the *NME* Brat Bus tour.

JANUARY 19: On Campus at Sunderland University with live sets from Terrorvision and China Drum. We always looked forward to doing the On Campus nights. They were an occasional series of live gigs from Student Unions round the country, where we'd get to do the show out of London (good), and get to put on a couple of bands (also good), and then bond as a team after the show by getting hammered (dangerous). China Drum, who I'd always had a soft spot for since their debut single 'Simple', gave us a guided tour of Sunderland in a mini-cab.

FEBRUARY: Interviews included The Stone Roses, Louise Wener from Sleeper, Belly and a chat with dEUS who also played acoustically in the studio. We also had Elastica in for four nights running – asking them questions about other members of the band. If you remember the TV show *Mr & Mrs*, it was like that. Among the snippets of trivia we forced out of them were such facts as: the favourite group of Annie, the bassist, was The Clash (or The Stranglers); guitarist Donna was a huge *Brookside* fan; Justin, the drummer, didn't bother with underwear; and one of singer Justine Frischmann's uncles wrote the Benny Hill theme tune!

FEBRUARY 7: Launch of Sound City in Bristol with The Bluetones and Gene. We launched this year's Sound City with a warm-up gig featuring two of the bands who we'd first played on the *Sesh*.

FEBRUARY 23: On Campus in Liverpool with Echobelly and AC Acoustics. I remember this for two reasons. One, Jo and I had agreed to DJ afterwards. That meant after the gig had finished, we spent the next hour behind the decks trying to work out which Pulp tune was the most dancefloor-friendly. Also, just as we had done in Sunderland, we hung around the following day to take part in a Radio 1 sponsored pop quiz. *The Evening Session* team came fifth (but it would have been much worse without Whiley's knowledge of Roxy Music).

MARCH: Another four-nighter with Radiohead to mark the release of *The Bends*, the album that was to take them to a new level both musically and commercially. There were veiled comments about how difficult the record was to record – and how the constant touring provoked by the global success of 'Creep' had taken its toll on them.

Jonny Greenwood: "It's like writing a play and then having to tour it for too long."

Thom Yorke: "We got to the stage of becoming acutely paranoid in the studio. There were times when we could have walked out of the studio and just given up there and then."

Other interviews featured Apache Indian (who was a very nice fella), James Lavelle from Mo Wax Records and Martin Carr, to trail ahead to…

MARCH 23: On Campus in Cardiff. The Boo Radleys. The Boos on the back of their biggest hit, 'Wake Up Boo', played live, less than a fortnight after scoring their first Top 10 hit.

APRIL 17: Sound City.

APRIL 26: Paul Weller plays live on the show. They made a TV trail for *The Evening Session* out of this, cutting together clips of Weller rehearsing at our Maida Vale studios. Jo, producer Christine Boar and me preparing for the show back in the studio:

Christine: "Paul Weller live. Apparently he's in a good mood."

Me: "Paul Weller in good mood shocker!"

Cut to Weller laughing.

MAY 4: I'm on holiday for a week. Jarvis Cocker co-hosted the show with Jo. I got a tape of this from Phil and it's a brilliant show:

Jarvis: "That's Bernard Butler – it's out on the 10th. Two days after VE Day. And he's playing the Hannover Grand soon… Watch out for them bouncers at that place – I had a terrible time the last time I went there."

And again (after playing '(White Man) In Hammersmith Palais' by The Clash): "I went to Hammersmith Palais the other night, but it's like *The Hit Man And Her*; I was very disappointed. Coming up next, The Stone Roses."

MAY: We also did our first interview with Supergrass, plus the return of Teenage Fanclub. Oh, and Black Grape. I wasn't quite sure what to expect from Shaun Ryder. I'd never met him before, but he turned up with Kermit, fresh from the pub round the corner, carrying a pint of Guinness. Their promotions girl even delivered the empty glass back afterwards.

Ryder (on the end of the Mondays): "The last three years of the Happy Mondays was like a relationship where you were going to bed with someone and not having sex. I always thought we could fix things, if we just had some time off. But people were more concerned with big dollar than music. I did fight for the Mondays to stay together. Go away for a year and come back, but everyone else wanted to finish it."

"So how did you get together with Kermit?" (formerly of the Ruthless Rap Assassins).

Ryder: "Well it was just me and him. We didn't have any friends left. No one would talk to us."

"Have you swapped musical influences? What does Shaun play you?"

Kermit: "Rod Stewart."

Ryder: "Early Rod!! When Rod was a mod."

JUNE: Jo's turn for a holiday, so we phoned round to try to find some guests and no one was in the country (or at least that's what they said). Instead, I came up with a new phone interview. "If they're not in Britain, then they must be on tour, or something. So let's phone the bands up and ask them: 'Where are you right now?'"

Guests in the studio – who were in the country – included The Chemical Brothers (chatting and mixing) and J. Mascis from Dinosaur Jr. (not chatty).

JULY: We'd played a couple of records by a band called Perfume who we both liked – and it became a running gag that Mick (their singer) shared his birthday with Jo. Without her knowing, we got hold of Mick and set up Whiley live on air. She was interviewing him over the phone from his rehearsal studio – or at least that's where he claimed he was. In fact, he was standing outside the studio door. Halfway through the interview he walked in, carrying a birthday cake. Candles and everything.

Other July highlights included a series of last half-hour mixes (from, among others, David Holmes, Fluke and the team at the dance magazine *Volume*), plus interviews with the Roses, Garbage and Peter Buck from REM, which I recorded at their gig at Milton Keynes Bowl.

AUGUST: A whole bunch of stuff. Jo did Ash (bassist Mark Hamilton was so nervous, he had to leave and Jo started again with singer Tim Wheeler); there was me with Money Mark; and a Charlatans interview made up entirely from questions we'd received from listeners. Oh, and the big Blur interview plus the first play of tracks from *The Great Escape*.

SEPTEMBER: Manchester In The City.

OCTOBER: Guests included Green Day, Menswear, Jarvis on the phone again, John Power from Cast and Brit-rap outfit Kaliphz. Then, just as we'd gone to the spiritual home of the New Wave Of New Wave, we now decamped to the spiritual home of Britpop.

OCTOBER: Camden Live.

NOVEMBER/DECEMBER: Sleeper, Kim Deal on the phone and Chris Evans.

Chris Evans. There's a name that is writ large in Radio 1's recent history. Although, in fact, it wasn't where I first met him. In-between working for *NME* and doing a stint on Q102, I helped out on Gary Crowley's Sunday afternoon show on GLR. No one used to be in at GLR at the weekend, so you could learn how to edit tape and mix in one of the spare studios. And after a while I started contributing a weekly London gig guide.

If Crowley – before the days of XFM – was the indie sound of Sunday afternoons, then Chris Evans was the anarchic wake-up call of Sunday mornings. I only heard about the final six months or so, but it was one of the few radio programmes I've ever taped (it was basically Chris, and a few listeners who'd been hauled in to the studio, having a good time). Some of the features, like 'Personality Or Person?', later reappeared on his Radio 1 *Breakfast Show* – which had an almost instant effect on morale in the building.

Having spent a year being part of a network that was being constantly berated in the press for losing listeners, the staff at Radio 1 had adopted a kind of trench mentality. Before the benefits of Matthew Bannister's changes had started to emerge, the atmosphere was tense and occasionally gloomy.

Evans changed all that. There was a certain amount of resentment about his show being produced by his own company, and how he often flouted the playlist rules and so on, but in his first year there he had the place buzzing. Or at least he did on the *Session*. It was like watching your team sign a new striker who immediately started banging in the goals left, right and centre (he struck the first on his opening morning when he played 'Welcome Home', the new theme tune for listeners who were returning to Radio 1).

I've tried not to use too many music–football analogies in this book (though there's quite a few, I can assure you), but this one seems appropriate somehow. I've stood on the terraces at Colchester and watched as we've sunk down the table and the home crowds have dwindled. And I've been there again, when a new bunch of youngsters have broken through and the entire team seems to respond. But it's not just this image that makes me think of Evans.

I could always tell who the most talked-about DJ on the station was, just by having a drink in a pub called the Drury Arms before a Colchester match. As soon as Evans started, everyone wanted to ask questions about him – or talk about something he'd said on air during the week. It was during one pre-game drink (with Steve Green and Ian Gerry) that someone said, "You should get him on your show," and promptly collapsed laughing.

It wasn't a bad idea, though.

There were other good reasons to be seen alongside each other at the time. Evans, with *The Breakfast Show* and *TFI*, had started championing several bands we'd played on the *Session*. He even used to phone up during the programme and swap stories about records we all liked. For a time, *Breakfast* at 7 a.m. and the *Session* at 7 p.m. were like the bookends of the day. So when Jo took another break, we broached the idea with the bosses, and Evans said yes.

Me: "It's Lamacq and Evans and that was Black Grape, and Chris have you come tooled up?"

Chris: "I have come tooled up… I've got two bags here. I've got a Tesco's bag and a Crispin's Food Hall bag. And in this bag, because you've got to have respect for *The Evening Session*, I've got half a bottle of warm cider, ten Embassy Regal, and for some reason there's bits of card ripped off the top of it, don't know why. I've got a copy of *NME*, *Viz* and *Marxism Today*. And that's it…"

"And you've also brought some records with you, which we're going to play, and here's the first one, and why?"

"Oh, it's The Pursuit Of Happiness and it's called 'She's So Young'. This is simply the best pop song I ever heard in my life. It was never a hit. By a Canadian band. But it's also got the best gap. The best way to get anyone to listen to the radio is to stop talking… silence. [Pauses for three seconds.] And then everyone goes, 'What was that?' Stuart Copeland from The Police once said that the most important beats are the ones you don't hit… and I think that's quite profound as well. And in this song, there's a beat they don't hit."

"Aah. But is it a better gap than the one in 'Should I Stay Or Should I Go?' by The Clash?"

"Steve, it just doesn't compare. Just wait till you hear it…"

Apart from the warm cider and the gaps in records, Chris did his 'Personality Or Person?' quiz on the phone with Andy Cairns from Therapy? (where celebs are asked questions about everyday life, to see if they've turned into a personality or they're still a normal person). Mr Cairns was deemed very much "still a person".

The co-hosts didn't stop there. Other guests invited to present the programme around this time included Underworld, Fatboy Slim, Tim Burgess, Zoe Ball (while she was presenting *Live & Kicking*)… and, erm, Ant & Dec (off the back of a really pretty good pop single called 'Better Watch Out').

With them killing time post-show, before going to catch a ferry to Belgium or somewhere for more promo, we decamped to the pub where – and I'm not sure how this came up – they suggested, amid gales of laughter, that I should remix their forthcoming single 'Shout'. I know this much about remixing. And that's not even the size of a postage stamp.

But, true to their word, the duo's record company at the time phoned up and we went off and booked a studio in South London for eight hours on a Sunday afternoon/evening. They sent over the DATs and, during a mild panic, I persuaded an engineer called Kenton to do all the technical stuff. Come the day, I arrived with some scribbled notes, told him I wanted lots of guitar on it, and we turned the track into something approaching A Tribe Called Quest's 'Can I Kick It?', only with a jungle beat.

They put it somewhere on CD2.

CHAPTER 22

King Of New York

One afternoon, around the time of Madchester, in a massive hotel near Times Square, Factory Records boss Tony Wilson offered the American record industry a fight.

Not a physical one. Not a punch-up on the sidewalk between a gang of British indie labels and some well-turned-out American corporate types. This was a fight over creativity and invention. This was about artistry and honour. This was the cunning and playful boy on holiday goading his American cousin over his lack of culture and subtlety.

It's folded now, but there used to be an annual music event in America called the New Music Seminar. At night, New York's venues used to rumble to the sound of bands trying to impress record labels and journalists, and by day there would be a series of crushingly dull discussion panels called 'A&R Of The Future', 'Breaking New Territories In The Southern States', 'AOR Formatting For The Under Fifties'. And all the seminars had guests sitting on a top table and all the guests were high-powered execs called Brad and Bill and Hank.

Representatives of the British industry used to go to NMS – as they still go to its latter-day equivalents like South By Southwest in Texas – to try to work out how the hell you sold records in the States. The Americans flocked from every state to see who could talk the loudest and give out the biggest number of business cards in a week. I'm surprised that there isn't a bell that sounds every so often in the background ("Brett Guzzelwitz has hit 100 cards today! Let's hear it for Brett!"). And yes, this is stupidly cynical, and smacks of xenophobia, but during our lives we will all have American friends we like and business acquaintances at whose mention we shudder.

Over the years I've met some extraordinarily nice folk in the American music and media game (but even they would admit that if you want to find the brashest, loudest, scariest creations in the biz, then America's the place to go – the PR people and the radio pluggers, well, some of them really are straight out of *Spinal Tap*). At times in the eighties and mid-nineties, you even got the impression that the American industry was like a National Park, set up to protect some of the ghastliest creatures of the seventies.

And this was what had got up Tony Wilson's nose. The Americans were slow and out of touch. Worse still, they weren't buying any of our records (The Stone Roses had recently returned from America with their tails between their legs, and Wilson's Happy Mondays weren't faring any better).

So, Wilson – a respected man, who later set up his own British version of NMS called In The City – went to New York, and called *his* panel 'Wake Up America. You're Dead'.

The hour-long session started very positively, if it was a little dull. Wilson and his guests explained how Britain was in the throes of the house music invasion (which ironically had come from Chicago). Britain was also cross-fertilising dance and rock genres and had bands who were the real deal and fell into their record label offices after 24 hours clubbing. It was exciting and the scene was changing. But what was happening in America? Wilson argued that the States was ignoring the most exciting music on its own doorstep (again, the house producers and scratch DJs) in favour of adult-oriented rock dinosaurs.

What turned the mood of the room, however, was a sudden outburst by comedian Keith Allen, co-opted onto the panel by Wilson and determined to shake some life into the proceedings.

Acting out a role as a drug dealer – and eulogising over the effects of ecstasy on music – Allen riled up the onlookers to the point where some of the hip-hop representatives at the back of the room were ready to end the discussion physically.

And as the arguing turned to shouting, and the shouting turned to swearing, I wasn't there. I was supposed to be there (to cover the panel for *NME*), but after ten minutes I'd snuck out to meet an old friend from Brixton who had a flat nearby and was going to put me up for a couple of days.

When I heard about the panel's chaotic finale later that night at a gig, I went white. I was usually very conscientious about the job – but now I was going to have to explain to the headmaster why I'd been bunking off. I spent a day working on good excuses… and then, wandering round the seminar's reception area, I came across a stall that sold cassettes of all the panels. "Can you do me 'Wake Up America. You're Dead'? By tomorrow?"

"Certainly, sir, that's the most popular one this week."

Tony Wilson had been in the game long enough to know about the friction between labels in Britain and the States, but I was a novice. I couldn't believe some of the stories that A&R people began telling me about how transatlantic politics affects the careers of new bands. Was I really that naive?

Try this, for example. It's going back many years (so the system may have changed, I'm not sure), but one A&R man told me that each year his label invited their counterparts from America over to Britain so that they could sit in a huge boardroom and play each other tapes of their recent signings. The American reps would yawn through the British bands, and then, having got the hump, the British reps would do the same to the Americans. Later in the year, the Brits went to America – and they repeated the whole process.

And I don't know whether this rivalry, this communication breakdown, was down to ego or insecurity. It could just have been that they didn't understand each other, because there was – and I imagine there still is even now – a complete clash of cultures at times. In the early nineties when the British band Five Thirty were being entertained for the first – and, I think, only – time by their label in America, one of the staff took them to a table-dancing club. As they sat and fidgeted, they heard one of their own songs come over the PA and cringed with embarrassment as various scantily clad ladies stripped off to the accompaniment of their song, which the A&R man had slipped the club DJ some money to play. They returned to the UK, incredulous.

Numerous other bands will have stories like this. And, to be fair, there are scores of tales of British bands embarrassing themselves in America. No one has prepared them for the assault course that is an American tour, with its eight-hour drives and promotional merry-go-round. It's hard work.

So when bands talk about breaking America, I think about this and wonder whether – having paid for the ride – they'll want to get off halfway through.

The British bands of the nineties – our *Evening Session* favourites – had their own share of ups and downs. Radiohead's 'Creep' was a huge anthem that turned them into an overnight success story in America. But it also dubbed them 'that Creep band', and when *The Bends*, their second album, arrived – defiantly un-'Creep'-like – they suffered commercially.

Elastica and Oasis both did pretty well for a time. But Suede, Pulp, Blur – the most English of the Britpoppers – all struggled, just as countless other Brit bands had struggled before them. Never believe one of those headlines that says 'X BAND TAKE THE STATES'. They've *been* to the States. I'll give them that. They may even have played ten dates in key cities. But in most cases America refuses to be taken anywhere. It's stubborn like that. It's big and immovable – and doesn't have much time for our sensitivities and our subtleties. It likes graft.

It wants to see you on the treadmill. And you better bloody well be polite while you're about it. But this is why some UK artists used to fail, and also why a band like Coldplay succeeded. From the moment they got their first break, Coldplay followed the U2 blueprint of touring America whenever possible (U2 used to go three times a year – one tour of the east coast, one of the west, and the one everyone dreads, the arduous and challenging one straight through the middle).

For some British groups, though, who've done one tour of Britain and been made deities overnight, this reality comes as a terrible shock.

Back in the mid-nineties, with Britpop sales booming, America stopped mattering so much to people for a while. So what if our bands weren't making it there? Let's face it, even the American groups we were championing couldn't get arrested in the States. And they lived there.

Which was actually pretty true. Perversely, in the middle of the Britpop era, the *Session* got behind a series of unlikely American bands. First Rocket From The Crypt, then two groups who went on to make the Top 40 with their debut British releases. The first came early in 1996. I'd been employed to make a corporate video for EMI (I know, all very Alan Partridge – that's all I thought about all day). The job involved interviewing members of staff so they could explain the different departments of the company to new recruits.

Down in the offices of Chrysalis, I bumped into their head of press, who told me about some new American signings they were going to launch in a couple of months. She gave me a CD and it lay around at home for a couple of days and then I played it... and it was so out of step with what was going on in this country that it was brilliant. It was SO American. And that's how we tripped over the Fun Lovin' Criminals. We did our own edit of 'Scooby Snacks' for the radio, and we banged it in the programme the following night, even before a release date was set. In fact, the label went with 'The Grave And The Constant' as the first release, but by August 1996 they followed it with 'Scooby Snacks', which hit the Top 40.

Very sweetly, when Huey Morgan from FLC was in town prior to the release of their second album, he called to say: "I want you to have the album from us. Not from the record company. I want to deliver it to you in person. I'll come round your house..." He never did. But it was a nice gesture. And they've repaid our support on several occasions over the years. But already there was a theme to the American groups who were popular in the UK. Apart from Green Day (massive on both sides of the Atlantic), Rocket From The Crypt didn't mean much in the States, despite signing a massive record deal, and Fun Lovin' Criminals couldn't even get arrested outside their own apartment.

The same was partly true of our next tip. We saw out 1996 with a curious album that arrived in the post one dour, rainy morning from America. I remember it was pissing down because the record seemed to capture the mood. I was on a mailing list for Geffen Records in the States (a result of having met A&R man Mark Kates, who was the guy who signed Elastica in America). Geffen had already given us Weezer, whose 'Blue' album we'd embraced enthusiastically, and then came this band called Eels. Bear in mind, I have absolutely no idea who Eels are, or where they come from, or why they were signed. I haven't got a clue that singer E has already released two solo albums, or that some radio station in New York or LA or wherever has been playing them so much that they've started to attract attention from various labels.

I know ZIP. And sometimes that really helps. British bands, with their press packs and their A&R buzzes, come with all manner of preconceptions and emotional baggage. *Beautiful Freak* just came out of the blue. It was one of my favourite records of the year.

And at the time it probably sold 14 copies in America.

America-related trivia break: It's a bit cheeky, I know, but when we used to have bands playing live at our Maida Vale studios, there was a button in our studio which let you eavesdrop on what was going on (without the band knowing that you were listening). Just before crossing to Green Day's debut live appearance, Jo and I listened in – and they were playing along to all the records on air. You should have heard their version of 'Kandy Pop' by Bis.

Me: "So you've been recording the session today… is this new material or stuff you can find on the album?"

Billie Joe: "Two of them are on *Insomniac*. It's the single 'Brain Stew', 'Jaded'. And also two others called 'Do Da Da' and another one called 'Good Riddance', which is previously unreleased."

Me: "You're not going to do what you did last time, which was to record a brand-new song and then get the engineer to ditch it."

Billie Joe: "Yeah, he erased everything. Actually that's when I found the title for the song. I was going to the bathroom and that's where I saw the words Armatage Shanks and that was what we called the song."

Me: "You named a song after a toilet."

Billie Joe: "Yeah."

CHAPTER 23

For The Dead

Having felt poorly for months, Britpop was finally taken to hospital in 1997. The poor thing. People were fighting over its will even before it had passed away.

I didn't go to the funeral. I hate music scene funerals; they're a bit of a mess. You get a bunch of critics turning up who you haven't seen for ages ("Sorry we had to meet again under such unhappy circumstances"), then the vicar makes a speech about how Britpop or grunge or Madchester will be sorely missed, and then the record company execs shove off back to the house and nick all the free food.

As Britpop lost its fight for life, there were a lot of people left very upset. I spoke to one promoter in Sheffield who'd just put tickets on sale for a big-ish band of the time and it was clear after just a week that it was going to stiff. "When did Britpop die?" he asked down the phone. "When did *that* happen?"

Last Tuesday. Just after *EastEnders*.

Meanwhile, the major labels had invested in countless groups who had done very little apart from burn a hole in the corporate cashflow. And there was uproar in the press. I've never seen anything like it. Not only was Britpop a goner – but several experts claimed it was the end of rock'n'roll, full stop.

Bless them. Here, have a nice cup of tea and a sit down.

You wouldn't find this sort of hysteria in other industries. Farmers see crops fail because of bad weather – and agreed, some of them will sell up and try their luck elsewhere – but you don't get headlines saying 'Farming's All Over' or 'Is Farming Dead?' Crops succeed, crops fail, crops succeed again. (I've suddenly realised you can take the farming analogy much further. Is the change in trends just a form of crop rotation?)

The problem with Britpop was that it had got out of step with the laws of supply and demand. At the start, there were a handful of bands who hit the charts, and as the weeks flew by the appetite for Brit-guitar music grew and grew. As the first wave of bands disappeared to make new albums, they left a gap in the market. All those hungry new Radiohead and Elastica fans and nothing to feed them.

So the majors started running round signing anything that moved (or, in some cases, anything that simply breathed or could hum in a cockney accent). On a bigger scale this time, it was a repeat of the A&R feeding frenzy that followed in the wake of Happy Mondays and The Stone Roses, when virtually every band in Manchester was scouted at least once. Sadly, for some labels, they were so late on the uptake, however, that by the time they arrived, they were left metaphorically scavenging in the bins.

The Manchester music regulars became so miffed by all this that someone even started a fanzine called *If You Have To Dial 061 You're A C– – –.*

I'd like to, but I can't blame the major labels for everything that started to go wrong in 1997. Some of the bright young things who were signed in the initial 18 months of optimism simply didn't flourish as expected (because there will always be groups who, for whatever reason, never fulfil their potential). And anyway, some of the indie labels had gone just as barmy.

But by the time the Britpop leaders returned to the fray, there were simply too many groups looking for too few places on the playlist or for picture stories in the press. The business plan was all to cock; the supply outstripped the demand. Overnight we were faced with a Britpop mountain. Scores of bands were simply left rotting by Camden Market.

*

There were some dreadful mistakes and miscalculations being made. Faced with stiff competition, labels turned the Top 40 into some kind of arms race.

They started releasing records on multiple formats, and then discounting the price of them to make them more appealing than the rest of the pack. They spent thousands on co-op ads with the major High Street record stores (a co-op is a deal that gets your record high-profile space on the shop's racks and a mention in the store's advertising).

The money they were spending didn't seem to matter at the time. British music was the talk of the town, and the bank accounts were looking healthy. But the majors were well on course to outspend their income. And when the audience woke up, and realised that some of the identikit Britpop groups weren't really going anywhere, that's when it all came to a grinding halt.

As a brief aside here, it's always puzzled me how the big companies deal with plummeting record sales. Around this time, there were copious articles about the rise of video games at the expense of album sales. Yet faced with accusations that CD albums were overpriced, the industry never once tried to tempt audiences back by lowering the cost of CDs in the shops. Oh, there were mid-price reissues and special offers from time to time, but nothing more. That was so typical of the level of arrogance in the business up to the nineties.

Back in the Square Mile in Camden, there was panic on the dealers floor. It was like the Wall Street Crash or the Hong Kong Bank (and, of course, everyone was looking for a Nick Leeson to blame, so you had to watch your back the whole time). Just as one sniff or a rumour about a fall in profits can send a company's shares plummeting through the floor, just one whisper of a disappointing midweek (an Echobelly or a Menswear) sent a band's reputation reeling.

How many times in the summer of 1997 did you hear the phrase: "So and So. They're all over"? But it wasn't all over. Just like the tide had gone out on the New Wave Of New Wave, leaving Elastica behind, so it went out on Britpop, but there was still Oasis, Radiohead, Blur and the return of The Verve striding up the beach.

Mind you, if the tide was going out here, it must have been coming in somewhere else.

I've referred to Manchester countless times in this book, but it's important to point out the contribution to pop music of Glasgow as well. If Manchester often led the way with mainstream alternative pop music, then Glasgow – on countless occasions – has been Britain's DIY dynamo. In the eighties it had Postcard Records and Aztec Camera and Orange Juice. Then came Creation Records, McGee, The Jesus And Mary Chain and the Primals (not to mention The Soup Dragons, who later scored huge hits on both sides of the Atlantic, the wonderful Teenage Fanclub, and the influential Pastels and Vaselines, to name but a small handful).

Away from London and Manchester, Glasgow – well, Scotland in general – was full of all sorts of interesting bands who were being nurtured by the John Peel show. Scotland overturned the fi: from Britpop's hi to the next generation's lo. If Britpop had been played out in the mainstream, mostly by the majors, then the latest wave of Scottish groups were defiantly independent. In 1997 we got the gorgeous 'Lazy Line Painter Jane' by Belle & Sebastian. There was Mogwai, The Delgados and their Chemikal Underground label. And from the same stable there was Arab Strap.

For years, the Strap held the record for the most consecutive plays on *The Evening Session*. Their debut single, 'The First Big Weekend', was played on every show for two and a half weeks.

The only record that came close at the time was 'Rockafeller Skank'.

CHAPTER 24

Punk To Funk

Iknow this might come as a shock to you – unless you grew up in a small corner of Essex – but I used to run the Equinox Disco. Well, co-run actually. It was Carl Daw, the electronics whizz-kid from my physics class who actually did most of the graft. It was Daw for a start who bought two turntables from a Tandy catalogue and then set about making them look like a proper Citronic Disco unit. I was very impressed. Two decks and a mixer (like the ones they used to advertise in the back of music weekly *Record Mirror*).

We spent another afternoon making and painting two lights boxes – the sort of sad-looking traffic light affairs that you find in village halls – and then we were ready. We had our own mobile disco. Stuck for a name, we trawled through Carl's record collection one afternoon looking for something snazzy to provide us with inspiration. Sadly, as all his singles seemed to be by Jean-Michel Jarre, we were limited to the French pioneer's output of *Oxygène* or *Équinoxe*. I reasoned we could always change it later.

But that's how the Equinox Disco started (we dropped the final 'E', I seem to remember, which would make for a good gag here, but you're probably ahead of me on that one). Before long we were out every fortnight playing wedding receptions, youth clubs, friends' parties – and even my old primary school. The decks used to break down at least once every three gigs, and the speakers blew one night, but mostly we were as professional as it was possible for two 14-year-olds to be.

In retrospect, this was the first time my DJing ambition had got the better of me (although I rarely said anything over the mic, apart from "Last orders at the bar"). As well as the pile of Jean-Michel Jarre releases, we put the cash from the gigs back into buying records, collecting a stunning array of dodgy compilation albums and a few 12-inch singles. All of a sudden, though, I found I'd turned into a musical schizophrenic.

These days when, happily, music is far less tribal, this condition isn't a problem. In fact, it's a positive advantage. But back in my teens there were endless drawbacks caused by an allegiance to more than one brand of music. How could you be punk, for instance, if you had a Chic record at home? How could you be a sensitive indie type interested in poetry and New Order when all you could recite was a list of varying beats per minutes (Donna Summer 'Hot Stuff' 138, Edwin Starr 'Contact' 132... and that's just off the top of my head).

I've kept remarkably quiet about my dance addiction over the years, but every so often it just blurts out. Did you know that the amazing 'Shame' by Evelyn 'Champagne' King – a record I still play at home occasionally on a Sunday morning – was the biggest-selling 12-inch of 1978? Or that, before they had a hit with 'Oops Upside Your Head', The Gap Band released a better record called 'Baby Baba Boogie' (my first ever import purchase from a shop in Bournemouth)? I suppose the reason I've decided to get this off my chest is that, like all those eighties indie bands who jumped on the dance bandwagon with appalling baggy remixes, 'there's always been a dance element to my music'.

So while we're in confessional mode, here are two words: Norman Cook.

It had been a quiet fortnight at the *NME* and the only feature I was due to write was a small introductory piece on a new – and much-tipped – Scottish band called The Trashcan Sinatras.

Their press officer duly sent me a cassette of some new songs and I duly listened to it at home one morning, scribbled down a few questions, and then put the kettle on.

In the background, the Trashcans' songs ended and the tape flipped over automatically to reveal something very un-Trashcans-like indeed. Instead, the tune on the B-side was a loping, mellow dance number with a girl singing prettily over the top. Must be a cock-up, I thought. Actually, hold on, whatever it was that wasn't the Trashcans was quite good.

On further investigation, the only words printed on the B-side were Beats International. Who the hell were Beats International when they were at home?

Back in the office, the phone call to the press officer went something like this: "Thanks for the Trashcans stuff. By the way, who are Beats International?"

"Oh, that's Norman Cook's new thing."

"Wwwhhaaattttttt?"

Norman Cook? One time bassist with The Housemartins? The last time I'd seen Norman Cook in the flesh, he was bouncing – and I mean, really bouncing – around the stage at the Hammersmith Clarendon. The Housemartins had started life as one of the fanzine world's favourite groups (the ace *Cool Notes* had written about them all the time, including the band's 'Adopt A Housemartin' scam where fans could offer floorspace to the group to kip on after dates on their first tour). They'd gone on to have number one hits, but then, at the height of their fame – just after the tabloids outed them for being middle-class lefties – they split, publicly and somewhat acrimoniously. There had been stories of the four members wanting to go off in different musical directions and there had always been rumours that Cook was a soul boy at heart, but nothing had quite prepared me for this.

"I think we should do something on it," I spluttered. "Let me see what I can do." And so the tape went round the office. Cook, it transpired, had stayed with Go Discs Records – home of The Housemartins and also new signings The Trashcan Sinatras – and was ready to make a comeback. The feature was commissioned and I ended up on a train heading towards the south coast.

Cook lived one station short of Brighton (there's probably a gag here too) in a house that boasted not one but two playrooms. The first was indeed full of kids toys; the second, a small box room upstairs, was full of shelves weighed down with 12-inch singles and old vinyl LPs. This is where he had been since The Housemartins split.

"Rocking backwards and forwards on a stool in the living area of his new house – upstairs there's a small home studio and a Scalextric – our Norm's got a new 'bonehead' haircut but has held onto his boyish smile," the subsequent feature divulged.

Cook revealed that he'd worked on numerous dance remixes since The Housemartins split. But had he felt insecure since the band broke up?

"Yeah, definitely, because of the switch to dance music and because I thought people might think I was jumping on a bandwagon. But then when I started doing a lot of remixes, most people buying the records didn't know I was in The Housemartins. Or they didn't know who they were.

"I take your point about being a white bloke moving into dance music, but this is what I've been interested in ever since I was 14. And after a while doing remixes – and seeing people dance to them – I realised I'd almost rebuilt the whole track and that gave me confidence to make my own records."

The new one by Beats International (the loping reggae one featuring guest vocals by ex-*Grange Hill* actress Lindy Layton) wasn't a conscious effort to take reggae back into the charts. But it was designed to halt a landslide of incorrigible headlines.

"I suppose it was a reaction against the pun 'From Housemartin to Housemaster'," he said.

'Dub Be Good To Me' was also an attempt to "do something completely unhip".

"The bass line on the single is an affectionate tribute to The Clash. It's like me tipping my cap to them because they were a huge influence on me growing up, both musically and politically."

I pushed him a bit on this, trying to see if he would admit to nicking the bassline of The Clash's 'Guns Of Brixton' hook, line and sinker. But no, he maintained: "It's a recreation of the original."

I might have sounded sceptical about this – or about the new Norman. I don't know. But all of a sudden he added: "You should get out of the indie guitar ghetto, Steve. Dance music's where all the new ideas are happening."

By the time the feature hit the streets, 'Dub Be Good To Me' had started making inroads on radio, too. It subsequently went to number one. That was the last I saw of Cook for ages (apart from a surreal live appearance with Freak Power at the T In The Park festival one year). I hid the ticket out of the indie guitar ghetto under my bed and forgot all about it. After all… he'd never be able to pull off another shock like that.

By Christmas 1996, with the music scene becoming restless, it was obvious that the mainstream needed freshening up.

It was a time of upheaval for me, too. Lisa I'Anson was leaving the lunchtime show, and, having been a hit with her *Saturday Social* programme, Jo Whiley was approached to take over while I'Anson took maternity leave. The original plan was that Mary Anne Hobbs would replace her on the *Session*, thus reuniting the *NME* Two for the first time in four years. We got as far as trailing Mary Anne's arrival on a show over Christmas – but just before the change round, Chris Evans quit *The Breakfast Show* and there was a snappy rethink. Mark and Lard moved to breakfast, Mary Anne took over their late-night slot, and I was given the nod to go solo on the *Sesh*.

If that wasn't scary and foreboding enough, just two weeks before Jo left the show, I split up with the Better Half after seven years. And then I promptly contracted conjunctivitis. For the first two weeks after Jo's promotion I was doing the show squinting through one eye.

Partly by luck and partly through judgement, we tried to galvanise the new *Session* into action by broadening its musical horizons. Big Ant from Collapsed Lung had already started tipping me off about some new dance and hip-hop tunes, and the more I looked around, the more the maze of dance music led me into new and often very exciting territory. It was long overdue for me.

Other people had been cross-fertilising rock and club culture for years (Underworld, for instance, whose 'Born Slippy' was the perfect crossover tune at the time). Plus, the band that the tastemakers were talking about back then were not your average indie-thrash band but were a duo who had grown out of an indie-thrash band. It was Bentley Rhythm Ace. Armed with this scant amount of knowledge and £50 from the cashpoint, I went shopping.

One of the records I bought in a spree at HMV was 'Punk To Funk' by Fatboy Slim, which I'd never heard but thought might be worth a go because: a) it was on the interesting Skint label; and b) it had the word 'punk' in it. What a sucker, eh? I loved it. It had a sample of *The Big Match* theme tune on it and we played it the following night. I played it at the wrong speed, mind you, but if you listen to it, it sounds better at 45 anyway.

A day later a man from the promotions company came on the phone.

"Heard you played Fatboy Slim."

"Yeah, good record."

"It's Norman Cook's new thing."

"Aaaaaaaarrrrghhhhhhhhh."

And the rest, as they say, is history

Note: Norman Cook grew up to take over the world. At the *NME* Awards in February 2000, he won best DJ. And I shook his hand. And I thanked him for his advice.

CHAPTER 25

Happy

We squabble over whose idea it was, but between us (Jason Carter and Matt Priest from Radio 1's promotion team and me) we came up with the idea of taking *The Evening Session* on tour.

Mark and Lard had just been on the road with *The Breakfast Show* and with their covers band The Shirehorses entertaining the student masses of Britain. So when it came to planning live events for *The Evening Session* for 1998, the idea of taking the team on the road for a week was virtually staring us in the face. What was more exciting was how we'd do it.

It took an hour of brainstorming to plan, but by the end of it Matt and I had the blueprint. We'd hire a proper, Starcruiser-style sleeper bus and build a studio in it. Then we'd put a tour together with three bands and follow it round the country. Sleeping on the bus.

I was grinning from ear to ear. Sleeping on the bus. Like a band on tour. Really travelling round the country SLEEPING ON THE BUS!

In my head, the idea of *The Evening Session* tour wasn't based on Mark and Lard's at all. It was fuelled by a week I'd spent on tour with the band Therapy?. Back in 1996 I had the same agent as the band, and after a drunken night at a gig in London, they'd asked me to DJ between bands on their next set of UK dates.

The tour started with two nights at the Shepherd's Bush Empire and then we were off for another six days. I learned all you need to know about tour bus safety and etiquette in about ten minutes from Roger Patterson, their tour manager. For future reference, the advice was:

- Always sleep with your feet facing the direction of travel (that way you won't break your neck if the coach stops suddenly).

- Don't use the toilet.

- Try not to get a bunk too close to the recreation area – people in bands will stay up all night drinking and watching videos and keeping you awake.

- Don't leave half-drunk cans of lager where they'll come a cropper as the bus goes round a roundabout.

And that's it. I mean, really, these are the only rules.

So by November 1997 we had the concept. All we had to do was book some bands, and book them sharpish, so we could get the tickets on sale before Christmas.

Travis were on board immediately. They'd just had a minor hit with 'Happy' from their debut *Good Feeling* album, but also they'd endeared themselves to *The Evening Session* a month earlier in New York. We'd taken the show to the States to cover CMJ – the big annual college radio festival that had replaced the New Music Seminar – which every year embraced a handful of 'showcase' gigs by British bands anxious to attract attention in America.

Travis played two shows. One was a terrifically upbeat set in a bar in the middle of nowhere. The other was their proper seminar show where they shared a stage with, I think, Mansun. The second gig was swamped with people from their American label, one of whom came out with one of the most extraordinary sentences I think I've ever heard at a gig. Now, I know American radio pluggers are meant to have a sense of the absurd about them (see *Spinal Tap*'s Artie Fufkin for more details). But having worked the room, the guy sidled up to singer Fran Healy and, putting his arm round his shoulder, said: "OK Franny, great gig. Now let's go shake some hands and kiss some babies."

On the whole, Fran didn't look like a man who wanted to either shake hands or kiss babies, but he followed the plugger anyway.

So Travis were in (because they were nice, quite gregarious chaps, and because if we needed any babies kissing, then we had the man for the job). To co-headline, we chose Catatonia. And I pay respect here to the judgement and terrible singing of then *Session* assistant Hannah Brown. It was Hannah who had started regaling the office with renditions of Catatonia's single 'I Am The Mob' – and the enthusiasm rubbed off. The more I listened to it at home the better it got. On the back of that I wheedled myself an advance copy of *International Velvet* and that was it. Done and dusted. I'm hit and miss with my predictions, but there was a track on it called 'Mulder And Scully' which was going to be the next single, and that was a nailed-on Top 40 record. No mistake.

Besides, it felt like Catatonia's time. They'd managed to hide in the corner during Britpop, and now all the scuffles had died down, they'd taken this as their cue to re-emerge. They had a cracking album up their sleeves – a mixture of hook lines and sensitivity – and they had Cerys Matthews, who was Nancy from Oliver.

It's strange putting this on paper now, but back then, as 1997 wilted away, they felt like the natural progression to what had gone before in the past three years.

Idlewild, meantime, who I booked to open the show, were something of a curveball. I'd been on my way to the Garage in Highbury one night to see a group called Astronaut but had half an hour to kill so I popped into the Hope and Anchor in Islington on the way to see them. They'd just released a seven-inch which we'd played a couple of times on air, so it made sense to see what they were like.

And that was about the only thing that did make sense. The bassist leapt around like a maniac, bashing his head on the low ceiling, the singer was intense (or possessed) and grappled with his hair a lot, and all the while they made a noise that was a great, angular pop racket. The audience – all friends of the headlining band – looked on bemused but applauded politely at the end of each song. It was like watching Seymour all over again (by coincidence, the only other music industry people in the audience that night were Matthew from Food Records and the group's future manager, Bruce Craigie).

I saw them again at the Garage a few weeks later, this time with Simon Williams.

Me: "Great aren't they, but do you think the kids will get it?"

Si: "Nope."

Me: "No, me neither."

I booked them for the tour and Simon released their next single, 'Chandelier'.

Now, I'm not a connoisseur of tour buses, but boy did ours looked impressive. It was silver and had 'Evening Session' in huge letters down the side.

The bus was hired from a company called Nova Travel, who also supplied Brett, the driver. Brett's opening speech revealed that he had even fewer rules for his vehicle than on the Therapy? bus: "Only one rule. No dumping. Every form of vice and sin is fine, but no dumping."

And it was in this playground den that we went to work. And it's here that you'd expect a blow-by-blow account of all the testosterone and tomfoolery, but if there's one thing I've learned about touring, it's that retelling the stories is the hardest and most unfulfilling part of it all. Touring comes with several in-built mechanisms for ensuring that it remains just that little bit elite and mysterious. Namely, the in-joke! The short-term memory loss! The stuff that you do that's so out of character you'll never want to tell people about it until you're on your deathbed.

And anyway, who's really interested, if every story you tell either starts with the line "It was really funny, right..." or finishes with "Well, I guess you had to be there."

I think this is why bands who've just come off tour are listless and irritable and make no sense. Apart from suffering from the obvious lack of attention – let's face it, no one cheers when you walk in the pub, like they do when you walk on stage – they have nothing to say. Nothing that connects them to the real world. All they have is a bunch of crap jokes, a few stories about their guitar tech and his underwear, and an impressive array of service station knick-knacks.

Not only that, but my most vivid memory of this tour was the journey across the Snake Pass from Manchester to Leeds, which isn't very rock'n'roll, is it? All it was was a gang of colleagues on a bus telling stories and talking nonsense as Simon Mayo crackled out of a transistor radio and we gazed at the scenery. Maybe it was something to do with the fact that, by then, we all felt comfortable enough to take the mickey out of each other mercilessly? Maybe it was just that slightly fuzzy feeling you have after two or three late nights?

Who knows? Everyone on the bus probably does, but I'll be buggered if I can explain it.

For the sake of future pop historians, though, here are the more accessible highlights.

DAY ONE: Glasgow Barrowlands. Belle & Sebastian – all 108 of them – record a live acoustic session in our studio on the bus. Meet Fran Healy's mum. After the gig Travis try to break into our bus because they've run out of beer and they think we have a secret stash. They do this in the dead of night in their pyjamas.

DAY TWO: Manchester. *Melody Maker* arrive to do a feature. Tell them that we had to saw two seats out of the bus to get all the studio equipment on board. They describe conditions on the coach as "like being in a U-boat".

DAY THREE: Leeds. A day off for the bands, but we take the bus on to Leeds and park outside the venue, the Duchess, where The Pecadilloes are playing. Burn an incredible amount of money in the pinball machine and after the gig get woken up by a posse of drunks trying to rock the bus about.

DAY FOUR: Birmingham. Fuzz Townshend, ex of Pop Will Eat Itself and now Bentley Rhythm Ace drummer, turns up and busks on the bus. This entails a very long percussion solo on a drum kit we've made out of various bits of debris we've found on the bus (eight empty Pringles tubes and a Tupperware container that used to have some spare fuses in it). Post-gig, hold an impromptu after-show party on the bus with Fuzz, Cerys Matthews and assorted fanzine writers. Halfway through, we spot one of Idlewild trying to snog someone in a bush.

DAY FIVE: Newport. Roll out of my bunk to find Radio 1 soundman looking down at me laughing. Go and check in a mirror and understand why. Best gig of the tour. Am given a pair of Welsh flag boxer shorts by Cerys (just one example of the underwear she's been bombarded with for the past week. Thinks. Does this make her the new Tom Jones?).

DAY SIX: London. Home. Bored.

A year later, in May 1999, we did it all again, this time with 3 Colours Red, American all-girl band The Donnas and a very young version of Muse, who I booked at the last minute on the back of their debut EP and who turned up – for their first ever British tour – in a lurid orange, double-decker tour bus. Unkindly, *Kerrang!* magazine described them as being "disappointingly anaemic when sandwiched between the two other bands". This is Muse, who have since won 7,493 *Kerrang!* Awards and are regularly voted Best British Live Act. Well, they had to start somewhere.

The main difference this time was that the team were all boys. The staff on the show had changed (Claire and Hannah moving on, and Rhys Hughes, Simon Barnard and Joe Harland joining).

Rhys 'Chunky' Hughes was used to touring. He'd been in bands, you see, not that he liked talking about them. NOT MUCH. Every town we pulled in to, Rhys would crane his neck round and peer out of the window to see if the venue we were going to was one he'd played before... Actually, that's a terrible exaggeration. But then the second *Evening Session* tour was all about exaggeration.

It is a strange thing, but people on tour play to character. Loud people are louder, sick people are sicker, and messy people are even messier. On the second tour, without even thinking about it, the boys from the *Session* – me included – played out our real-life roles with a certain panache. Simon needed to sleep more than ever, and looked like he might break when he eventually raised himself from his bunk of a morning. And Joe, the efficient one, was unbelievably more efficient and organised than ever – except on the day we drove to Sheffield and his thirst got the better of him. Fortunately it was Saturday, and a day off, and after starting on the Bacardi Breezers in Manchester, we arrived in Sheffield where Joe climbed onto the roof of the bus and promptly fell asleep sunbathing.

The two of us ended up going to see dEUS and Ten Benson at the excellent Leadmill, though when the gig finished and the Step On club began, I lost him again. Getting up onto the stage to try to survey the room, I spotted him in the middle of the dancefloor, headbanging to The Offspring.

For my part, I did everything I always did (went to bed too late, got up too early, ate nothing but curry and crisps). If I wasn't such an exaggerated character on tour as the rest of the team, then that was simply because I did all this at home anyway. It wasn't as if I'd been let off the leash.

But in some cases I think that's why people go barmy on tour. It gives them a chance to behave in a way they can't at home or in an office. So scarily, although people talk about bands being juvenile on tour, I'd hazard a guess that the characters they portray on the road are probably closer to the real them than the parts they play in polite society. And if that's true, then that's quite frightening.

Mind you, I can think of one thing that was MORE frightening. And that was producer Rhys's snoring. Rhys had come to the *Session* from Mark and Lard's *Breakfast Show*, via a stint on Simon Mayo's programme. His most recent stint on tour had been as bassist in The Shirehorses – who, along with his girlfriend – had completely failed to warn us about the noises he makes while he's asleep. AND I HAD THE BUNK OPPOSITE HIM. You know in cartoons when a character is snoring so heavily that the sheets on top of them rise and fall in time with their breathing. That was Rhys.

But despite this, we got on terrifically well (along with Alan and Kev, the on-board Radio 1 engineers, who are always the funniest part of any outside broadcast – years of setting up sound for everyone from Radio 5 Live sport to *Sunday Night Is Music Night* have imbued the Beeb's technical staff with a gallows sense of humour second to none).

This time round we invented a feature called the Tour Trauma League Table, giving and taking away points depending on how much of a turbulent time the bands were having on the road. The Donnas won it, despite Joe's loyal attempt to win bonus bravery points for the *Session* team by climbing out of our bus and onto the roof as we sped down the motorway. He'd have made it as well, if the rest of us hadn't grabbed his legs.

This is my funniest moment of the 1999 tour, though. Simon had been given the task of taking The Donnas shopping in Manchester. The only problem was that it was pouring with rain when they were supposed to go. So, as the band sheltered on the steps of the university on the Oxford Road, Simon – who's been unable to hail a cab – spies a bus coming down the road and darts out to the edge of the kerb to make it stop.

Unfortunately, The Donnas haven't a clue what he's doing. And Simon's neglected to tell them. The bus stops, Simon jumps on, and then just as he turns round and the doors close behind him, he sees The Donnas, standing exactly where they were, giving him a blank look. The bus pulls off and he gesticulates at them, hopelessly – four damp teenage Americans in an unfamiliar city.

Five minutes later, having jumped off at the first stop he could, the next they see of this man from the BBC is an out-of-breath, out-of-shape, skinny short-haired indie bloke running back up the street desperately waving at them.

Later in the year I went on tour again. But this time it wasn't with a band. This time I WAS the band. And I know I've said all the stuff about not being a frustrated musician, and never wanting to be on stage. But honestly, this is different.

When I joined Radio 1, my friend Tony suggested that we get a booking agent and see if he could fix me up with some DJing dates round the country. Tony used to drive, and we'd turn up at Student Unions and indie clubs and play some records and I'd mumble into a mic and shuffle about looking embarrassed every time I cleared the dancefloor.

But with some practice, and experience, I started to find it was possible to mix records, rather than just segue them, just as it was possible to clear a dancefloor and refill it. ("If you're any good," Jez from Utah Saints once said, "you don't worry about clearing the floor because you've got records up your sleeve that will pack it again.")

In the spring of 1999, I went to said gig agent – a chap called Jim Morewood at Helter Skelter – with the idea of maybe taking a week off work and doing a tour of Student Unions during freshers' week. Jim thought this was possible – in fact, Jim was very good to me over the years, and only really cocked it up once when he suggested that I did an NUS conference in Reading.

The theory was right enough. Every year the NUS puts on a weekend of showcase gigs, so that the various entertainment officers from around the country can cast their eyes over some of the groups who agents are trying to promote in the following term. If I was DJing, who knows, they might even book me. That was the theory.

The reality, though, was that on the coldest, wettest, most miserable day of the year, the gig took place in a marquee outside the Reading Uni building. Every time a band went on, a handful – and I mean a handful – of people would wander in, take one look at their breath frosting up in front of their faces, and head steaming back to the sanctuary of the bar. Meanwhile, I had to DJ on a door-sized raised platform to one side, that thanks to the rain was surrounded by a small moat.

I've never let Jim forget this. Nor did my friend and driver Liam, who has wafted through life doing various jobs involving increasing amounts of proper responsibility (although he did once run a gym where he worked with Spice Girl-to-be Geri Halliwell). Liam is lethal. He could poke a student in the eye with such deft precision that you'd think he'd been trained by the SAS. In fact, dressed in his combats and woolly hat, you'd think he *was* one of the SAS. Anyway, Jim came up trumps with the tour and we set off for the opening date in Bath. It was coldest, wettest, most miserable night of the year. And when we arrived we were shown the marquee.

This tour taught me a lot about what it must be like when you're a new band on the bottom rung of the circuit. Me and Liam stayed in small B&Bs – mostly twin rooms to keep the cost down – and had to work out our journeys so they didn't clash with rush hours, which turn into traffic jams, which in turn sap your patience and resolve.

We'd already noticed other similarities between ourselves and the lives bands live on tour, of course. We had our own in-jokes that nobody else understood (mostly quotes from the film *Mars Attacks!* or various editions of Chris Morris's radio show *On The Hour*); we had our favourite service stations up and down the M1; and we were so hyped up after a gig that to go straight back to the hotel and hit the sack was absolutely unthinkable.

We were also affected by the same outside factors, like being at the mercy of the promoter's fly-posting budget, or being given maps to the venue that were drawn in 1975, 18 years before a new one-way system was introduced. But, of course, it was still a tour – and at ten days, it wasn't long enough to send us insane. I think I could do two weeks without seriously damaging my health, but how bands manage four-month-long treks across America I'll never know.

CHAPTER 26

High Noon

By the time Oasis prepared to release their third album, *Be Here Now*, they were the most sought-after band in Britain.

Radio, TV and the press were fighting over any little scrap of news or information about them, and behind the scenes there were endless negotiations over which TV channels and radio stations would get the 'exclusive' first play of tracks from the record. For the promotions team who were working Oasis, it was a delicate balancing act – not helped by the fact that a copy of the first single from the album, 'D'You Know What I Mean?', had leaked out to a local radio station in Scotland.

The pluggers had promised the first play to Radio 1 but were caught on the hop. It wasn't their fault – but it mucked up their carefully laid plans. At *The Evening Session* we were told we'd get the album first and could play as many tracks from it as we wanted. A day later, the plan changed. We could have three tracks one night and another five the next.

Then on the day we were ready to broadcast the first three, Oasis's people called to say that I had to talk over the start and end of every track – or better still drop a Radio 1 jingle in the middle of them. Now, I could see the management's point here. They were scared of bootlegs of the songs creeping out to Camden Market and across to the States before the album's official release. We were also entering an era when albums had started leaking onto illegal download sites, which would become a massive bugbear for the industry in the following years. However, there was no way I was going to play a jingle over the middle of a song. I just didn't feel comfortable with that at all.

The trouble was that we'd already promised the listeners that they'd be able to hear the album in its entirety, based on the original plan. Now we had to go on air and backtrack, play the three tunes we had been delivered, and promise the rest on the following night.

Come the next day, the remainder of the tracks failed to show. According to the plugging company, Ignition (Oasis's management company) were unhappy that I hadn't talked over the tracks enough. I'm still not sure whether this was bootleg paranoia gone into overdrive or whether there was more to it than that (pressure from Oasis's American label Epic, maybe?). But I ended up back on air, apologising to listeners again for not coming up with the promised goods. We got a further two tracks, but that was it. It was a messy and not particularly enjoyable couple of days.

At the end of the campaign, a rumour went round that Noel wanted to break his radio silence. It might happen tomorrow, we were told, or next week. Who knows? Are you interested? Considering the grief that had gone before, I suppose we could have just gaily waved two fingers at them. But then again, wouldn't that have just been a case of shooting ourselves in the foot?

Because, despite everything that had happened, the letters from Oasis fans had far from stopped – and anyway, Noel Gallagher is a great interview. He's funny and he never dries up on you. He'll maybe try to get one over on you, depending on his mood, but he's never dull. What we hadn't factored in was the possibility that he would turn up with Liam.

This was a bit of history. The brothers hadn't conducted a high-profile interview together since the 'Wibbling Rivalry' showdown for *NME* back in 1994. The news of Liam's appearance spread like wildfire round the Radio 1 building. By the time the brothers arrived in the studio a small crowd had already formed behind the glass partition that separated my studio from John Peel's.

I'll admit I was a little unnerved. Possibly a little apprehensive.

But Noel and Liam loafed in and I shook hands with Noel. Then I put my arm out to shake hands with Liam, and he simply looked down and stared at it.

"You're shaking man. Why are you shaking?"

You should be standing where I am.

As they sat down, Liam carried on: "So who are you shagging then?"

Sorry?

"Who are you shagging at the moment?"

Me: "Erm, well, no one. I don't know, sometimes you're so busy you don't have time to start a relationship… that's what I find."

Liam: "Are you saying me and Patsy are fucked?"

The CD machine that's playing is counting down the minutes and seconds of the track that's on air. It says 1 minute 27 seconds as Liam gets to his feet again and offers to punch me out.

Noel: "You've took it the wrong way, man. Sit down."

Me: "I didn't mean *you* don't have time. I'm saying that when I'm working flat out, that's when a relationship suffers."

Liam: "Right. 'Cos anyone says that me and Patsy ain't going to make it, I'll take them on."

The CD starts to fade.

Me: "It's *The Evening Session* and that was 'Fighting Fit' by Gene."

Listening to the interview for the first time in nearly three years, they sound far more wasted than I thought they were at the time. It later transpired that they'd spent the afternoon at the *GQ* Awards (a fact that everybody neglected to tell me at the time).

The interview starts politely enough (there's some small talk about the band having just returned from America).

Then comes a fairly innocuous question about the B-side for the forthcoming single 'All Around The World'. And then Noel lurches to one side and says: "We've actually recorded a cover of 'Street

Fighting Man' just to piss Keith Richards off because he's been slagging us off."

Piss I can handle. I don't even notice it whistle through the air. Then, from out of the corner of my eye, Liam starts to fidget.

Liam: "Can I just interrupt here?"

Noel: "Interrupt away."

Liam: "All these slags coming out of the closet at the moment right... before we go any further, I'm going to shoot me mouth off to them right..."

Noel senses the danger even before I do. Standing up, he produces a wodge of cash from his trouser pocket: "All that says you'll shut your mouth. Go on, what is there? £85? And a platinum credit card."

Liam: "No, I've got my own, man. Listen right, all these old farts who get out the day centre, they've got a problem with Oasis. And I ignore all that, right? Because I dig their music, but at the end of the day they all must want a scrap, right, and I will offer them all out right here on radio. So if you want a fight, right... Primrose Hill Saturday morning, 12 o'clock. I will be there. I'll beat the fucking living daylight shit out of them. And that goes for George, Jagger, Richards and the other c– – – who gives me shit."

Noel: "So in answer to your question: yes, we have just been to America."

There is a sort of unwritten league table which deals with swearing on air at the BBC. The first time I knew about this was when the band Menswear were recording a session for us and asked the engineer how much they had to censor the lyrics to their song 'Stardust'. Without a flicker of emotion, the man at the mixing desk looked up and said: "Shit OK. Fucker no good."

What about the C-word, though? A producer had once told me that one C was as bad as five Fs – in which case we were already scoring swearing points left, right and centre. Except no, maybe no one would have noticed it. Maybe that was the rant out of the way. Maybe not.

Me: "Who's hurt you most out of those?"

Liam: "Oh, fucking hell, it's got to be Jesus Christ, hasn't it? But no, listen, no one's hurt me, right? Because I still dig their music. But at the end of the day it's getting childish, innit. It's like being in the playground, and I left the playground years ago. Now they want to be pushed onto the fucking swings."

Me: "Do you think they say these things because they've been goaded into saying them by the press?"

Liam: "I think they're jealous and I think they're senile and they ain't getting enough fucking meat pies in them."

Not sure why, but I make a thoughtful "Mmmm" noise here.

Me: "But does it bother you? Because you're bigger than that."

Liam: "Yeah me, personally, I'm bigger than that, but they obviously want a scrap. And I will beat them up if they want a fight."

Noel: "SHUT UP, man."

Liam (sounding a little hurt): "What? I told you I was going to say that."

Noel: "NEXT QUESTION."

And so it continues. There's a celebration of the recent tour – including two dates in Aberdeen which they rate as among the best of their career – and their appearances at Knebworth. Then it's on to the changes in their audience, and the relationship between the brothers on stage.

Noel: "When he turns to me and goes 'Are you mad for it?' That's what it's all about."

Me: "OK, we'll be back with Noel and Liam after this from Laidback…"

Noel: "He's getting thrown out after this…"

We both tried. Producer Claire Pattenden and I both asked them if they could cut out the swearing. Noel was contrite, Liam seemed put out. Claire tried again, but Liam got up from his seat and looked suddenly very menacing. He wasn't having any of it.

Claire: "I'm the producer and asking you to tone it down…"

Liam: "Well, I'm the fucking singer in Oasis."

It's live radio. There's no delay mechanism. We have the two most famous rock stars in the country in our studio – possibly a bit pissed. I suppose we could have pulled the plug on them there and then, but at the time I never felt that was an option. Besides, this was the most animated I'd ever seen them. Who knew what might come out of the interview?

On my tape copy of the show, the tracks are edited out, but the next bit happens like this. I back announce the Laidback single and Noel talks about the hype surrounding the release of *Be Here Now*, blaming it on their label Creation. Liam falls silent. Then there's a minor verbal skirmish over whether it's the best record they've made to date – and I ask if it's the end of an era.

Noel: "Yes, definitely."

Liam: "He's right there. You're on the ball. You cleaned your teeth this morning. Flossed them maybe?"

Noel: "We always said the first three albums were part of one big one. It's the last Oasis album of the nineties. I'll say it to the kids now, there ain't going to be another Oasis album in the nineties."

Liam: "We're going to kick in, in the millennium… The next one, am I too far away from the microphone? I don't want you shouting at me. But the next one's going to have more colour in it. That's what I think. If I've got anything to do with it."

Noel (laughing): "But you haven't."

There's a Captain Beefheart track – chosen by Noel – and then we're into the news. I'm surprised we didn't get a mention ourselves. "Hundreds homeless after flood in India, but fucking hell, you should hear what's happening on *The Evening Session*…"

We come out of the news with a Paul Weller song and discuss the brothers' favourite bands of the moment. Among them are Ocean Colour Scene, Travis and, of course, The Verve, led by Richard Ashcroft.

Noel: "When he got on a stool and played a few songs before we went on in New York, including 'Bitter Sweet Symphony', now they are songs that do actually touch you… But I will say [slight pause] drugs do work."

Me: "That's something you've been quoted as saying before."

Liam: "Either that or he's got a shit drug dealer."

The pair dissolve laughing.

Me: "Is it good to have The Verve back then, so you've got someone to push you?"

Noel: "Listen, right…"

Liam: "He asked me the fucking question – will you calm down?… It's nice to have them around."

Noel: "There's only one person that's going to push Oasis on, and it ain't going to come from any particular band. It's to do with us. Now is Verve time and that's the end of it."

Liam: "I disagree. [Sounds hurt again.] It's our time."

Noel: "Well whatever. Richard is a genius. And Nick McCabe is one of the best guitarists I've ever seen. And even when we supported them years ago they were a great band then. And circumstances worked against them. I was the happiest man in the world when they went to number one with their album… He's not writing those songs for him. He's writing those songs for me."

Me: "How do you mean?"

Noel: "Because he's got to be a better songwriter than me, and then I've got to be a better songwriter than him. And that's what it's about."

Me: "OK, we're going to play another of the records you've brought in… DJ Shadow."

Liam: "Who's he? Is he a boxer?"

Noel: "Well, he's a shadow boxer."

Me: "That's such a terrible gag. We'll play this. DJ Shadow and 'High Noon'."

The DJ Shadow record kicks in… Not going too badly now, is it?

Me: "Talking of people who inspire you, do you still inspire each other?"

Liam: "Well, Noel inspires me – I don't know if I inspire 'im."

Noel: "Yes he does. He knows he does."

The sound of their voices has changed. They're more echoey. Not because they've moved away from the microphones, but because there are smoke alarms in the studio and the pair of them have been puffing away since they arrived. To avert the alarms going off, we've got the studio door held open by a chair.

Me: "Has your relationship changed over the last year?"

Noel: "Yeah. Of course it has, yeah. He's got more paranoid because he thinks the whole world is against him."

Liam: "And you're full of shit, because I don't think that at all. No, he inspires me, more than I inspire him. Me mum inspires me, me wife inspires me, me little stepson inspires me. Bottles of lager inspire me. You inspire me, Stephen, when you pay the time to listen to me."

Me: "But what is it? Is it the mood of the people around you that picks you up?"

Liam: "No, it's just people who can be arsed and who've got a brain and clean their teeth in the morning. People who actually listen to you and don't chop down everything you say. But listen, right, this chap hasn't been bed-friendly over the last couple of days."

Noel: "Bed-friendly? [Noel starts laughing.] What's bed-friendly? You ask my wife, I'm totally bed-friendly."

Liam: "No, I'm on about bed-friendly. Nothing to do with your wife. Anyway what was the question?"

Then the conversation collapses again. There's a question about the Oasis photo exhibition which was running in London at the time. Liam is definitely attempting to say something, but all Noel keeps repeating is "Shut IT. SHUTTTITTTT."

Liam: "I don't get anything out of the *expedition*..."

Noel: "Expedition? Where did you go marching to? The South Pole?"

Liam (smiling): "Shut up, man."

Me: "Apart from not being bed-friendly, you seem to be getting on really well."

Liam: "I'm about to knock the fucking c– – – out."

Noel takes the mickey out of Liam about the expedition slip-up.

Me: "That's playground behaviour, picking on your brother on air. I'm going to play another record."

Noel: "I'm allowed to! I'm allowed to!"

Liam: "Wait a minute, hold that record because I'm going to knock the c– – – clean out."

Noel: "He hasn't got a good enough lawyer to knock me out."

Liam: "I thought we were getting on all right till we came here."

Noel: "We were getting on all right. We do get on all right."

Liam: "But you've got a pen in your gob and it's pointing my way."

By this point we'd opened the phonelines to take questions to put to the band. And the enquiries (by both phone and fax) are piling up. Claire brings a bunch into the studio and we start on them after the next record.

Me: "Here's a question from one of the listeners… Will you start writing classical music when you get to 50 like Paul McCartney?"

Liam tears into this one: "Is Paul McCartney composing classical music? Because sitting around with a bunch of old lesbians doesn't sound classical to me. So no, we're not going to get into that pile of shit."

Then Noel gets defensive after I ask him about his visit to 10 Downing Street for one of Tony Blair's soirées at the height of Cool Britannia ("I didn't go there to represent some shit-kickers in Dagenham, I was going there for me").

Then we play 'There She Goes' by The La's.

Noel: "You have to understand, right, that when that album came out in 1989, everything was groovy and dancey and baggy. The climate was dance-rock-indie crossover and that was the first Britpop album."

Question from a listener.

Liam: "I believe in marriage and I believe in family. I'm going to buy a dog next week and I'm sorry if that pisses people off but I'm an old fart. [Brightening up.] No, I'm enjoying it. I wanna have kids, yeah, next year I reckon. Don't know. I'm going to have a bang at it."

Me: "Will you be a good father?"

Liam: "I'll be the best father in the world, yeah. I'll be shit at paying the bills, but…"

Me: "Has it made you feel less responsible for your brother?"

Noel: "He can look after himself. He's my younger brother, right… How old are you?"

Liam: "Twenty-five. And you didn't get me a present you c– – –. Oh, you did, you did."

Noel: "He's 25; I don't need to look after him. He's a bigger man than I am."

Liam mumbles something in the background about not needing anyone to look after him and says: "Don't speak for me, you c– – –."

Me: "Why?"

Noel: "Because he has to deal with his life and he has to deal with someone like me. But he's still a knob."

Me: "We'll play another track. This is what you wanted to hear by Travis." Off air, while the CD plays, we turn the volume up full blast and Noel sings along at top volume.

Me: "When was the last time you wanted to run away?"

Noel: "Gonna do it. We don't need a break, but I think people need a break from Oasis. Once we've toured this album, we have to sit down and think where we're going."

Bubbling away there's a disagreement over what Oasis should do next. Noel says they need a break, Liam – by now drifting off mic – wants to "get down to some serious work". Noel claims Liam loves being in the limelight. Liam disagrees. Vehemently. Liam wants to make another record.

Noel: "Well I don't. [Sounding suddenly very miserable.] Work's become boring, mate."

Me: "Suddenly you seem a bit down about it."

Noel (drawing audibly on a cigarette): "Yeah. Everything that led up to Knebworth was really special. Really exciting. Now we've become just another band."

Liam: "No we haven't. I don't know what band you're in…"

Noel: "We're going to take time off and regroup…"

Liam: "We're going to sit down and change the face of OUR music and like…"

Noel (interrupting): "Blah, blah, blah, blah…"

Liam: "Well see you later then…"

There is a tense silence as Liam stares at Noel and Noel stares at the floor… and then I hurriedly hit the Death In Vegas track 'Dirt'. While the record's on, Liam walks out.

After it finishes, Noel explains why he likes DIV, and I say, admittedly very belatedly: "It's Thursday night, *The Evening Session*, and if you're offended by any of the language on tonight's show… Turn off. That's our advice."

Noel laughs.

Me: "Here's another question which has come in. Has Liam ever written any songs and will Oasis ever record one of his tracks? Would you like him to write something?"

Noel: "I would do, yeah."

LONG CONTEMPLATIVE SILENCE.

Me: "And do you think he'd be good?"

Noel: "Well, we're talking about something I've never heard, so I don't know."

Me: "Does the responsibility of being the leader of the band ever get you down?"

Noel: "Well, yeah, it does, because, you see, it's like now. I always said that the first three albums were like one big rock'n'roll album. And I don't really want to go and do the same thing again, because that would be boring. It's not that the BAND have become boring or anything like that… [Lowers voice.] It's sort of not exciting any more. And HE would disagree, and I'm sure he's about to bound through the door at any second…"

Me: "Is it harder on you?"

Noel: "Well, we are the establishment, I understand that. And I don't know what I'm going to write next time, but if I can't do something that excites me, then I could possibly never do another album. But I need, mentally, time off. I could go and start to write another album next Tuesday afternoon, but it wouldn't mean anything to me, and I don't want to do that."

Me: "What do you do when you get down about it?"

Noel: "Well, I'm quite lucky because I've got a lot of friends in different forms of music. And I chat to them and they've got different ideas… and it's not like we're going to go and do a dance album. But I've said this since 1994, that the first three albums are part of a set and then it's going to change. And that's the most exciting thing. I don't know what the next album's going to sound like. And nobody else does.

"I want him when I play him the demos of the next album. I want him to tell me he's not going to sing it because he thinks it's naff. And I'll think, 'Well, we're getting somewhere now.'"

Me: "What was the band's reaction to the last album when you played it to them…"

Noel: "Well, as long as 'e likes it… When I'm sure about something, I'm really sure about it. And then I only need him to say, yes, you are right. He can sit there and say, 'Oh, I'm just the singer,' but it's his band… [And again more quietly.] It's his band."

Me: "You're getting…"

Noel: "I'm getting old now, Steve…"

Me: "Are you? Are you mellowing?"

Noel: "I'm getting fatter."

Me: "But you're giving Liam more credit than you've given him before."

Noel: "Well, no… um, yeah, I suppose I am."

Me: "Where's that come from?"

Noel: "I don't know. [First he sounds like he's about to cry and then he bursts out laughing.] He's got a good lawyer."

Me: "We'll play The Verve. This is 'Lucky Man'."

After The Verve, there's a chat about complacency, the music scene and Noel's proudest moments.

Noel: "One of the best things I've ever done is 'Setting Sun' with The Chemical Brothers. We're stuck in a rut of being this five-piece rock'n'roll band. Stick it in the Marshalls, blah, blah, blah."

Me: "You sound like you're unhappy with the last record."

Noel: "I'm not unhappy with the record. Not at all. I think the songs are great songs. But, I'll never record songs like them again."

Me: "OK, we have to wrap things up. It's the Sex Pistols. I read somewhere – it was in *The Sun* newspaper, I think – that this is your favourite album of all time."

Noel: "Well, *Never Mind The Bollocks*, I think I bought when I was 12, and it's still the most dangerous rock'n'roll record of all time."

Me: "Noel Gallagher, thank you very much."

Noel: "Thank you."

The show ends on 'Pretty Vacant' by the Pistols. Immediately we've come off air, there's a freelance photographer standing by to take a picture of Noel and me. Noel says: "You might get the sack after that…" Then it's all smiles for the camera. After Noel leaves, Claire and I and a couple of others decamp to the Stag's Head, where Gary the landlord has already pulled me a pint of a cider.

"Oh, mate," he says. "I was really feeling for you. I had it on in the pub, but then I had to keep turning the volume down when they started swearing."

For what it's worth, I thought it was a revealing interview. It was the first time Noel hinted that *Be Here Now* had been hurried and sounded like it was the end of an era (which, in retrospect, wasn't really the case). Liam said for the first time publicly that he was going to have children with Patsy. And Noel revealed there wouldn't be another Oasis album until 2000 (which *did* turn out to be true).

But, of course, you can't swear like this on national radio without there being some kind of furore. The following morning I stopped at the corner shop as usual and gingerly picked up *The Sun*. Sure enough: front page. '4 Letter Oasis In Radio 1 Shocker. Full Story Page 7.'

My stomach started to twist slightly. There on page seven, alongside pictures of the brothers leaving Radio 1, was the full story. 'Foul-mouthed Oasis brothers Liam and Noel Gallagher caused outrage last night when they unleashed a torrent of four-letter filth live on Radio 1.'

You have to admire the subs on the tabloids. Whoever had put the story together had done a very good Fleet Street job on it. As I skim-read the rest of the piece, all the key words were there: "disgraceful", "often rambling tirade", the references to drugs and the threats to Mick Jagger. It hardly seemed real. They'd even managed to get the necessary quote from an outraged lorry driver and another "appalled" parent whose 13-year-old daughter had "heard the Oasis row".

But it was the penultimate paragraph that really caught my eye: "Lamacq apologised for the swearing towards the end of the one and a half hour show – the most foul-mouthed pop broadcast since the 1976 TV interview which made the Sex Pistols famous overnight."

I was actually quite chuffed with that. Even if it did suggest I'd stopped being Someone Like John Peel and had become Someone Like Bill Grundy, the idea of causing such an extreme reaction excited every punk rock gene in my body. I never once believed it (the Pistols were on primetime TV for heaven's sake), but it was nice that someone had given us a context I was, perversely, quite happy with.

The problem was, I doubted very much whether the BBC would be as pleased. After *The Sun* I saw *The Mirror* (front page as well, but the full story and pictures included one of the posed BBC studio shots with me and Noel. What was that expression on my face?). The other tabloids had run with the story on inside pages as well, reflecting varying levels of indignation. One outrage creates another. Even the *Evening Standard* weighed in with a story peppered with quotes from a member of the clergy claiming that this was the sort of incident that was indicative of the declining moral standards of Britain's youth.

I imagine there was an inquiry. But it's telling of the time that although we were reprimanded (and the production team was certainly given a proper cross-examination), we survived relatively unscathed. Had the same incident occurred now, our hopes of still being on air a week later would have been much slimmer. The outrage aimed at the BBC would, I suspect, have been more powerful and more vindictive.

I'm honestly surprised, looking back now, that I was mildly oblivious to the fallout. In fact, I found out more about the incident reading Simon Garfield's book *The Nation's Favourite* a year later than I ever knew at the time.

There were even claims in the book, and which I've heard since, that actually it was this interview which finally, conclusively, proved that Radio 1 had thrown off its Smashey & Nicey image; that the stuffiness of the old guard had finally been consigned to history; that Radio 1 really was cutting edge.

I'm not sure if that's true. But I do know it's the most bootlegged programme I've ever presented.

CHAPTER 27

History

Noel and Liam were definitely right about one thing. It was good to have Richard Ashcroft around. I was a late convert to The Verve (so late that most of the pre-The days are a bit of a mystery to me). By the time I saw the light it was at their final gig at the T In The Park festival, just before they split for the first time. Ashcroft was spell-binding that night. He'd been wandering around the compound behind the *NME* tent for about two hours before they played. A tall man with a languid walk. He looked completely dislocated from the world around him.

By the time they played the tent was heaving. And for their part, The Verve were just really lovely. I know lovely's not a word you associate with rock critiques, but it was… lovely. The sound was big and tense and impassioned, but at the centre of the storm, it was almost as if Ashcroft was swimming to shore after finding himself shipwrecked. After they'd finished, he walked off the ramp at the back of the stage, barefoot, like he was walking onto the beach, and away from danger.

When they reformed and the tapes started circulating of *Urban Hymns*, it was clear they'd picked up from where they'd left off. Except they were even better (at least in some ways). Early fans doubtless missed the layered, claustrophobic rolling sound of their first records, but The Verve were song-based now.

I can't remember whether it was before or after *Urban Hymns* was released (possibly before), but they played a gig at Hammersmith Palais. This couldn't have been better for me. The Palais didn't book many gigs. But the times I went there were for special occasions. The first was the Ramones supported by The Prisoners (the night I bumped into Leigh from The Price on the balcony who said: "If The Prisoners start with 'Melanie' I want you down the front, sharp" – they did and I was).

The Verve gig was a hot ticket. After their split and subsequent lengthy absence, their legend had grown and grown. But it wasn't the new breed of fans that made the night so special. It was the followers who had arrived, vindicated for having faith in the group through all the bad times, who really made it a night to remember. The crowd reaction was extraordinary. By the end of the third song, the sea of applauding hands went right from the front to the very back wall. It was as if everyone felt part of some huge congregation – but at the same time there were people lost in personal worship. (One man, just to my right, didn't open his eyes for the entire gig. He stood and swayed and applauded and seemed to be plugged directly into Ashcroft's mind.)

Following the success of the album, their audience grew by the week, culminating with one enormous celebratory gig. The Haigh Hall show was to be their equivalent to The Stone Roses at Spike Island. I remember it, because it's one of the few times when I've actually felt part of a major event.

I got the 1.05 p.m. train from Euston to Wigan, and the compartment I was in was virtually reserved for members of The Verve's congregation. Opposite me, there was a couple of guys making their way to the gig from Eastbourne. Both former punk rockers (with a preference for Slaughter & The Dogs and Stiff Little Fingers), they hated outdoor festivals but thought The Verve were top. They also predicted that the heavens would open mid-afternoon and that we'd all be drenched long before the band arrived.

Behind them, I remember there was a troupe of younger fans whose stereos all leaked *Urban Hymns* and who spent much of the journey discussing the merits of the Super Furry Animals and

Spiritualised and singing Travis songs, in just the wrong key. I was late, so I got a cab at Wigan station driven by a 40-something guy who couldn't see what all the fuss was about: "They're not really from Wigan at all. They're from Skelmersdale, aren't they?"

"They went to college in Wigan."

"Yeah, but they lived nearer Skelmersdale. They're more Liverpool."

More Liverpool than what? Anyway, at least he thought the weather would be nice. He turfed me out about a mile from the site, amid scenes of absolute chaos. To get to the gig you had to walk down a winding country lane, which probably sees about six cars on a good day. Not with The Verve around, though. It was like a leafy Wembley Way, beer bottles strewn on the verges, and merchandise men trying to flog their wares on every corner.

And then when you arrived, it was through a gate at the top of the hill, which gave you an incredible view down to the stage at the foot of the rolling bank. All the BBC staff (radio and TV) were parked up to the right of the stage. This was a comparatively easy show to do. There were no pre-gig interviews to record. All I had to do was run through the script and work out a few links. I even had time for a bottle of beer with Cass from Delakota in the hospitality tent. The only pre-gig excitement was when a gang of ticketless fans charged the backstage gates and scarpered for the safety of the main arena.

The only difficult moment is the point just before the band go on stage. The record on air finishes, and you have to try to capture the scene you can see from the side of the stage. You're not sure exactly how long you've got – two, maybe three minutes, it depends on how much the group dawdle around.

I described the scene as best I could, feeling a little awestruck. The field was full to the back of the hill. You could just about make out a few expectant faces at the front. Just as I was beginning to fill for time, the cheers began. As with all these big gigs, it's the front few rows of people who catch sight of the group first – then the roar spreads through the crowd like a forest fire.

The gig itself seemed to pass by in a flash. The Verve looked assured, Ashcroft's eyes deep and dark and focused somewhere over the top of the hill. It was everything I liked about The Verve.

It was passionate but not pompous. They sounded big but not overbearing. They were in a good groove, rather than being in a rut. One thing about The Verve: I never once, back then, saw them going through the motions. Just like T In The Park, they played the gig like it was their last.

CHAPTER 28

Summer Here Kids

Phoenix Festival 1996: Neil Young is on stage. We can't go back to the hotel till Neil's finished. He has been on stage for what feels like three weeks. For the past two days he's being doing 'Like A Hurricane'.

A senior member of staff walks past just as I'm lying face down in the grass backstage by the BBC truck, pounding the ground with my fists and shouting: "For the love of God, somebody make him stop!"

So I've had some good times and bad times at festivals. We all have. Among the best and worst (in fact, possibly a mixture of both) is the year Radio 1 had us DJing at the T In The Park festival.

To be fair, it seemed like a good idea at the planning stage. The organisers of T In The Park, Scotland's first big two-day festival, asked if I could DJ on the campsite on the Friday night as people arrived for the weekend. The idea was that it would give people something to do, instead of simply roaming the site bored, or drunk, looking for their own ways of livening up the proceedings.

So this was OK. Between the T staff and Radio 1, they printed up some flyers and I duly arrived expecting to see a hundred or so people sitting around on the grass, waiting to listen to some music. Instead, looking up from the bottom of the field we were in, I could make out a large crowd pressed up against some barriers. And on the other side there was a tent that looked like it had been commandeered from a village garden party.

I'd invited a guy called Phelim O'Neill along to give me a hand over the four hours we were supposed to fill. And together we walked up the hill and set up on the tiny stage. I think I said "Hi" or something to the crowd and we started segueing a few CDs. And within half an hour the crowd had swelled to around 2,000 people. Two thousand increasingly drunk, mad-for-it people in a field at a festival. Where there was nothing else to do.

That's when the first beer can suddenly appeared out of nowhere and whistled past my ear, knocking over a pile of CDs at the back of the stage. Then came another. And another. This one half full. Then the can fight started in earnest. They weren't all heading at us; they were being lobbed back and forth between the crowd themselves.

"I'm not sure this is entirely good," I turned round and said.

"Nonsense," said one of the T In The Park bosses, "they only do this if they like you."

They must have liked Phelim even more than me, because two minutes later a three-quarters full can of lager whizzed through the sky and hit him on the forehead. He had to go to the Red Cross tent, leaving me on my own, just as Jason Carter from Radio 1 spotted four ambulances making their way up round the edge of the crowd. By now the police were estimating there was a crowd of 4,000 in front of us and wanted to pull the plug (even though the ambulances were apparently just a precaution and no one, apart from one sitting-duck DJ, had been injured). We made an appeal for calm and played Fatboy Slim, and slowly the number of cans in the air stopped a swarm of midges.

But the thing is, for all the fear of being hit (and believe me, that wasn't dancing up there, that was dodging and weaving), it was one of the most exciting gigs I've ever done. The man from the festival was right. Everyone did look like they were having a good time. Finally, after playing a few, slightly restrained Britpop tunes, it was time to up the ante again and hope for the best. I cued up

'Sabotage' by the Beastie Boys, hit the play button on the CD, and dived to the floor for cover. Literally. I hid on the floor behind the decks.

The whole field went nuts.

Phoenix Festival 1997: It's *Melody Maker* versus *Loaded* in the five-a-side football competition and we're holding them to a valiant 0–0 draw. *Loaded* magazine's team features several ringers in the form of ex-pro stars including then Coventry City boss Gordon Strachan. In goal for the *Maker* is one Steve 'The Cat' Lamacq.

Loaded are getting increasingly bored at not scoring, while The Cat saves shots with his knees, his elbow, and in one extreme case manages a tip shot over the bar with his ear. Honest. It hit me on the side of the head and went out of play. Strachan picks up the ball, beats two men, and BANG. As I fall over backwards, the shot cannons off my right foot and goes for a corner. We lost 2–0 in the end, I think, and got knocked out of the competition in the first round. Mind you, Strachan came over after the match and said, "Well played, keeper. Couple of good saves there." I was this far away from a trial with Coventry City!

Unfortunately, though I didn't know it at the time, I'd just broken my wrist.

I must have landed on it awkwardly saving Strachan's piledriver. After two hours wandering around the site watching bands, the nagging discomfort, turned to full-scale agony. At the Red Cross tent, a nurse gave me an ice pack to hold on it and they wiggled my fingers around till my face went red. As I was waiting for the ambulance to take a group of casualties to hospital, a chap in a suit came up: "Steve Lamacq? I'm from the *Daily Telegraph*. I'm writing a piece about a day in the life of the Red Cross at Phoenix… I was wondering if I could interview you?"

The hospital was miles away, somewhere in the direction of Warwick, but comfortingly it looked just like *Casualty* on TV. Only with fewer people.

A nurse handed me my X-rays and said: "We checked, and you've broken two small bones in your wrist. If you take the X-rays down to the room at the end of the corridor someone will put you in plaster and give you a sling."

They did. I got a cab. I made it back in time to see The Charlatans.

But here's a warning: British festivals can seriously damage your health! Think first. Most doctors don't go to Glastonbury.

I used to have just two rules in life. One: never go to gigs south of the River Thames. Two: never go to outdoor festivals. Live your life by these easy guidelines and you can't go wrong.

Except then I started going out with a girl who lived in Brixton. So ignoring gigs at the Academy, five minutes' walk from her house, would have been a little churlish. And then the *NME* finally persuaded me to review a day at Reading Festival. OK, I thought, but just this once. And now look what's happened. At a rough guess by 2018 I have covered somewhere in the region of 70-something festivals for the BBC – and DJed at countless others.

It wasn't meant to be like this. I had very strong reasons behind why I never went to festivals (I like gigs with roofs on and a Tube station within walking distance). Festivals, it struck me, were cold and wet and miles from the Tube and all you ever heard was the final strains of a band's set as it was whisked off by the wind and deposited in a ditch five miles away.

Then the war of attrition began, and slowly I lost the battle with festivals (so yes, you can get an OK sound mix, and it doesn't always rain, and you can live without public transport for a couple of days if you really try). But there's more to it than that. As a microcosm of the music scene, the summer festivals can tell you a lot about the pop landscape. It's one of the few chances you have to judge the comparative pulling power of bands, and their ability to move an audience.

You have to take into account that some bands are just simply no good at festivals – they're like people who are ultra-bright for the majority of the year but can't do exams. And then there are some groups who have made festivals their speciality. Still, as a rough guide to who's on the way up and who's on the way down, the festival circuit can be about as good as it gets for market research.

Not only that but the changes in the make-up of the summer festivals say much about developments in music over the past 20 years.

The terrific array of festivals in a summer season, which now seems to start in March and last until September, takes in festivals that cater for different genres and different age groups; festivals that use their setting as a selling point; and festivals that have mixed music with cars or food or science. Is there a festival concept that hasn't been done yet? Or a type of music that now doesn't have its own annual shindig?

My proper initiation into festival life happened in 1994 when I started compering the main stage at Reading.

This meant turning up early and playing music between bands – punctuated by occasional introductions, which involved standing at the side of the stage and shouting a band's name very loudly. My worst Reading nightmare was always that I'd forget who I was introducing. Or worse still, I'd introduce the wrong group.

The nearest I came was many years ago when I forgot who was about to play next – but I'd already started talking on the microphone. As I frantically looked for a running order in my pocket I manically tried to bluff my way through: "Time for more live music... please, welcome to Reading Festival 1998... a band who need no introduction... here on the main stage... make some noise for [huge sigh of relief] Fountains Of Wayne."

I've only ever really got into trouble once at Reading, in 1996. Having consumed too much alcohol the previous night, I struggled through the first part of Sunday before I went for a lie-down in the Radio 1 truck. God knows how long I fell asleep for, but I was woken by engineer Andy Rogers: "Steve! Steve! You've got some guests here to interview."

I had a vague recollection of arranging to interview someone.

In walked The Stone Roses. Fresh from a rather hostile press conference, they were here to introduce the new line-up, prior to headlining on the main stage (the now famous set where Ian

Brown's singing left something to be desired). Luckily I found some notes I'd made the night before, and the interview happened, and they sloped away again. However, during the sleeping/interviewing interlude I'd missed two introductions, clearly much to the annoyance of the stage manager. I've lived a pretty clean festival life ever since.

Clean, though, isn't a word I'd use to describe Glastonbury. Certainly not when it's raining. The BBC, as you might have noticed, is quite big on Glasto. My first one was in 1995, which was fine. I mean, it was beyond huge and completely incomprehensible to me, but I got the gist. And the weather was OK.

But then, after the fallow year of 1996, we returned in 1997 and for the first time I saw Glastonbury in the mud. The heavens had opened on Worthy Farm for most of the week leading up to the festival. Jo Whiley and I did a show there on the Thursday evening from an outside broadcast truck which was meant to set the scene for listeners at home – or en route to the event.

The scene we had to set was… damp.

"It's Thursday night, the *Session* live at Glastonbury," I said, in the style of a front-line news veteran. "And if you hear anyone saying that the conditions down here aren't really that bad… well, THEY ARE!" If the BBC ever needs DJs to broadcast during a national emergency, then here's my and Jo's phone numbers.

"Bring wellingtons. And straw. Make sure you've got something waterproof…" I trailed off. If we hadn't played a record, the next line was going to be. "Save us. Can anyone out there hear me…"

The BBC's operation – including radio and TV coverage – is so big at Glastonbury that engineers rig up what's been dubbed the BBC village backstage (including an on-air studio, a truck for recording all the live music, a tent for TV and an editorial portacabin). By day two of 1996 it looked like the set from *M*A*S*H*. The incoming wounded included live music boss Chris Lycett, who'd broken an ankle after catching it in a badly covered pothole.

Of course, it couldn't be as bad the following year... could it? No. It was worse. In 1997 it was just muddy. In 1998 it poured down.

As part of our brief, producer Claire Pattenden, myself and assistant Jo Tyler were sent out to the field where the Glasto organisers had erected a huge screen to show one of England's World Cup games. The field was rammed – the rain sloshed down. Jo held the umbrella, Claire the DAT machine and I had to vox pop the crowd about England's chances and what sort of Glastonbury they were having.

Making our way through the drenched mass of humanity, I pointed to a guy in the crowd. "He looks OK, let's try him."

"Excuse me, it's Steve Lamacq from Radio 1," I said as a drop of water formed on my nose. "How do you think England are going to do?"

The guy just stared at me for a second. Then at the DAT machine. Then back at me.

Then he said: "Steve? Are they really making you do this...?"

There are still some things that about festivals that I don't understand. Like why is festival cider always that bright orange colour? Like radiation-affected Tizer? It never is anywhere else in the world.

And why do people who've managed to avail themselves of free passes spend 90 per cent of the day sitting in the Nest Of Vipers? The NOV is what some of us have nicknamed the backstage bar area. Take Reading, for example. The Nest Of Vipers sits just to the back and to one side of the main stage, so all you get is a muffled sound from the back of the PA. I'm being harsh in my generalisations here, because obviously I'm aware of the benefits of only standing behind five people in the queue for the toilets and the fact that there are chairs and tables and occasionally polite conversation. But don't feel for one second that you haven't lived till you've been backstage.

I spoke to one festival-goer once who genuinely seemed to believe that the backstage toilets were fashioned out of marble and the champagne flowed like water, served by waiters with bow ties. It's not. It's not full of pop stars either (occasionally you might spot a bored American, who can't bear another minute on his tour bus doing the rounds, but that's probably it).

Nevertheless, I'm still in favour of introducing a backstage timeshare scheme where everyone could have 15 minutes to buy a drink and go to the loo. It just seems much fairer.

CHAPTER 29

Brothers And Sisters

"The most interesting work in any genre," explained horror writer Clive Barker, "is surely going to be on the perimeters, where definitions blur."

I can't remember where I read this, but I wrote it down on a piece of paper and found it in a draw the other day. It must have struck me when I saw it – as it does now – that it says everything you need to know about certain points in pop music. Although the centre, the mainstream, has the highest profile and generates the most sales, it's the stuff happening on the periphery that's probably more individual in its own way.

If the quote wasn't on a yellowing scrap of A4 – indicating it's a few years old, then Barker could even have been talking about the music scene at the end of the nineties (or indeed much of what's followed).

I have come up with hundreds of theories to help explain what's happened in pop music over the years (and a hundred more to predict what will happen in the future). Some of them, as you might have noticed, are scattered throughout this book.

I'm not sure if this implies that I have an almost OCD approach to rock, needing to rationalise and order my view of it, to the point where I can make a thing that never makes sense *make sense*. But, if nothing else, I suppose it does serve a purpose of sorts by putting bands and records and scenes into some kind of context.

The weird counterpoint to this is that I hate music that's predictable. I don't want pop to be a bunch of rules and theories. In fact, it's the total and utter lack of rules that makes it so interesting.

It's the completely arbitrary nature of success and failure which keeps music on its toes and gives it that level of unpredictability that makes it fascinating to watch. Imagine if there was a fool-proof formula for making hit records or launching bands. How dull would that be? No shocks, no upsets... nothing that wasn't beyond our control. It's almost too awful to imagine.

I know certain bands stand a better chance than others because of a whole list of reasons that aren't necessarily to do with their music or even their looks. Some bands come from fashionable towns, others have good managers or press firms or pluggers or mystery financial backers. But that still doesn't mean they're definitely 100 per cent sure of making it. And that's what's so great about the whole thing.

I've championed numerous bands who should have gone on to at least headline a tour of O2 Academies, if we were working to the idea of a definitive winning formula. And when they haven't, I've been mystified and miffed at the same time. But I love being proved wrong and then proved right and then proved wrong again. I love the way pop music is so erratic, and refuses to behave in character.

But I still do the theory thing because it's become a habit, and because one day one of them might work. And then I'll be jubilant and destroyed all at the same time.

My favourites are always about how music goes in cycles. About how you get peaks and troughs and watershed movements and you always get them in precise, recurring years.

I started with the mid-term theory. Every decade, somewhere in the middle, you'll find that pop goes through a massive facelift. It started with the arrival of 'Rock Around The Clock' in 1955 and continued in the sixties and seventies (when between 1975 and 1977 glam and prog rock were all but swept away by the emergence of punk).

Of course, this is baloney, and apart from the C86 movement, the eighties don't fit in at all (neither do the nineties, for that matter), but it was worth a try. Then there was the ten-year theory, which started with punk in 1976 and continued with the arrival of C86, the originally shy indie-pop scene that took its name from a compilation tape produced by *NME*... But this train of thought ran off the rails in the nineties as well.

In fact, it's the bastard nineties that did for virtually every rock blueprint I've ever dreamed up. Even the cunning 'Alternative Music Does Badly In The Charts During A Labour Government' theory ran aground under Tony Blair (though you could argue that in the same way that The Beatles were never the same after meeting Harold Wilson, Oasis were never quite as popular or rock'n'roll after Noel visited Downing Street).

My favourite of them all, though, was the double digit theory. This was a refined version of the ten-year gambit, again starting in 1955 with Bill Haley and the impact of rock'n'roll on the charts. Then you had 1966 with The Beatles' 'Yellow Submarine' and The Beach Boys' 'Good Vibrations', followed by 1977 marking the media arrival of punk and the Sex Pistols. The next one is a little wobbly, but 1988 gave us sampling culture and 'Pump Up The Volume' by MARRS, not to mention Chicago house, and the dawn of a new era around the Hacienda and Happy Mondays.

And then in 1999. Nothing. Or at least there was nothing I deemed worthy of including in the first version of this book, maybe because at that time, no one knew quite how big Coldplay were going to be.

From a commercial point of view, 1998 and 1999 were lean years for music; it was 24 months of sales stress and marketing madness. The money that swilled around during the Britpop era was starting to ebb away and the industry was slow to react. Labels spent too much money on signing bands which weren't a good fit for the mainstream, burdening them with massive advances they'd never be able to justify.

For the first time in the decade, there was no overriding or successful guitar scene to fall back on. But Barker was right about the material being made on the perimeters (although he wasn't to know, in the case of the music scene of the late nineties, that the bands on the edge would be so different to the world within).

If Britpop had been the centre of many things in the mid-nineties, then it had simply fallen out of the middle. Like a hole being punched in a Polo (except this time the record industry wasn't making a mint). Who could fill the gap?

The reaction to Britpop – the anti-Britpop, if you like – was musically inventive and experimental and in some cases far more ambitious and moving (see the rise of Mogwai and the post-rock of the late nineties, music which rejected Britpop's glibness). New indie labels had been springing up all over the country through the late nineties and seized their chance to ply us with caustic seven-inch singles, homegrown pop-punk and a poetic or lo-fi indie sound, typified by bands like Hefner, who took up residence in John Peel's Festive 50.

But none of this was going to plug the sales gap.

It wasn't supposed to. In fact, it was a marvellously liberating time, especially on *The Evening Session*, where we were heading more left of centre every week (with hindsight, much to Radio 1's chagrin), playing the nascent rock gods Muse and the baffling Ten Benson, Clinic and Flaming Lips, Guided By Voices and the aforementioned Hefner, who we even managed to squeeze, irrationally, onto a Radio 1 live gig supporting Stereophonics.

But obviously, someone still has to pay the rent. The charts reverted to boy bands, embraced dance music (some of it very good) and with little to offer in the way of resistance, welcomed a wave of American rock music that was variously described as nu-metal or rock rap (Part 2: the nightmare continues).

So maybe it's not surprising, in this general malaise, that the band to emerge in 1999, who would go on to become one of the biggest in the world, was made up of four awkward, unassuming college students, who wrote lightly strummed pop songs, set around a piano, and with a voice that sounded earnest and hopeful.

Coldplay had already been turned down by every record label in London by the time I first saw them on a wet Tuesday night at the Camden Falcon in 1998. They'd released the self-funded 'Safety' EP earlier that year, but the only interest in them came from Simon Williams at Fierce Panda and Caroline Elleray from BMG Publishing, whose tireless support kept them afloat.

And as I've said, I go to a lot of gigs. But it's very rare at the bottom level that you see a band who are 'ready'. You see bands who are like a can of beer you've shaken up before opening, all froth and fizz; you see bands who are excitable and nervous and all the more charming for it; and you see bands who will go on to be popular in nine months or a year's time. You hardly ever see a band that is 'ready'. But Coldplay were ready.

They were cocksure and bashful; cheeky but a little shy. They played to the audience (which was fine because they knew more than two-thirds of them from UCL, where they were studying). And they played some lovely songs, with some delicate guitar lines.

By the time they'd finished and I was standing outside with my friend Computer Mark – who I'd dragged out of the Stags Head in Fitzrovia to accompany me – we both agreed that this was something a bit special. The following week I tracked down the manager Phil Harvey and phoned him to offer the band a live session.

He phoned back the next day: "Sorry, we can't do that date. Will's got an exam."

We found an alternative date and the live session broadcast on February 25, 1999.

During the interview I said something like: "You had a single out last year which completely passed me by." To which Chris Martin replied, sharp as you like, with mock indignation: "But we put a copy in your pigeonhole… You didn't listen to it, you bastard!" (And then, under his breath: "We can't say that.")

They were terrifically friendly and charming and funny, while at the same time appearing to be constantly fretting about something or other. In the context of the time, with the roar of Fred Durst at the metaphorical door, they seemed completely out of sync. They weren't rock or Radiohead or even Travis.

No wonder the labels were dismissive of them. They didn't seem to fit anywhere. Mind you, I bet the A&R man who turned them down with the words "I just can't hear any singles in the set" is mildly annoyed with himself now (or at least should be).

They had *a lot* of peculiar, nicely crafted songs. Songs that hinted at disparate influences like Nick Drake, Radiohead and A-Ha and that came with lyrics that had an almost youthful, naive clumsiness about them. I couldn't help it. I was very taken with them.

To the point where over the next couple of years we'd book them for anything we could. They supported Catatonia at the Kentish Town Forum for some Radio 1 thing (where we had to send Cerys Matthews a CD so she could vet them). They did another support for us, opening for King Adora at the Harlow Square. And at least one more session, which was probably around the release of their debut album.

And all the time, their songs were out there starting to snag on the consciousness of the listeners. Jo Whiley hammered them on daytime; the *NME* put them on their annual January package tour; and in return the band gave us *Parachutes* and a massive hit single, 'Yellow'. Just the sort of record that would slot nicely into the hole at the centre of the pop charts.

I didn't spend New Year's Eve 1999 listening to Coldplay. I wasn't out in some dive bar, still scouting for the future of pop. Oh no. New Year's Eve 1999 I was at the Garage in Islington watching Brit-punk band Snuff. They split their set around the countdown at midnight and then launched into their version of 'Auld Lang Syne', during which I joined a stage invasion of happy revellers – the only time I've ever 'invaded' a stage. At one point I was standing next to drummer Duncan, who looked up, a bit shocked, and mouthed the words "What the fuck are you doing up here?"

I shrugged my shoulders. I don't know what I'm doing. Or where all this is going.

CHAPTER 30

The Modern Age

Leeds Metropolitan University, February 23, 2002. There are four of them on stage, wearing tunics, but bare-chested beneath. They are fast, frenetic and shambolic. They hash their way through a series of songs that fly by in a haze of amateurish guitar solos and rowdy choruses.

They are The Libertines. This is another game-changer for me.

Being as old as the hills, they, bizarrely, make me think of Britpop meets Eddie & The Hot Rods. They will go on to help fashion much of what happened to British guitar music in the noughties. Almost as much as the American band they're supporting tonight... The Strokes.

Just like there was, in the end, no Millennium Bug, there was no easy journalistic hook for us to hang our hopes on at the birth of the new century.

It was as if music was trying to tell us something. That the fracturing of scenes in dance and guitar music which had started to accelerate and become more prominent in the nineties would be a sign of things to come; that life would never be as simple again and that all the old blueprints, the routes to success which we once relied on, would be, one by one, put in the shredder.

Musically, 2000 was a breakthrough year for Queens Of The Stone Age and gave us a brilliantly volatile debut from At The Drive In, but of the American artists to really make an impact commercially, it was the year of Eminem.

And here I throw my hands up. If there were more hours in the day, or I'd bothered to listen more to Paolo Hewitt at the *NME* on the importance of late eighties hip-hop, then I'd be better placed to make some bold claims about the pivotal role of Eminem in redrawing the future of mainstream pop music.

But at the time, despite playing the records, I'm not sure we realised what a shockwave he was helping to create (and there, I guess, lay another strand of *The Evening Session*'s downfall). It would be a while before we properly reconnected with hip-hop (a moment of enlightenment, prompted by Radio 1 producer Sam Moy, which led us to book the first ever Dizzee Rascal radio session on *Lamacq Live*).

So we drifted through 2000, attempting as ever to reflect a range of music, including some good stuff from P. J. Harvey, Badly Drawn Boy and the excellent debut album from Doves. The only thing was that all these records, although great pieces of work, felt strangely grown up. They were crafted and literate. They were things of beauty and stature. But they weren't revolutionary.

I've always thought of Rough Trade Records boss Geoff Travis as being one of the most instinctive and impetuous people I've ever met in the industry. He is a man of obsessions or whims. He falls in love with groups on an almost weekly basis (which might be an exaggeration, but not much of one).

Sometimes the objects of his almost teenage exuberance are inexplicable. You look and listen and it doesn't make sense (we don't hear what The Travis hears). On other occasions, his understanding of rock'n'roll's joy, learned over a period of 40 years, is absolutely spot on.

So at the end of 2000, when he was rumoured to have found a new band from New York who would make the music press go weak at the knees, we sat up and listened. And sure enough, timed perfectly to take off at the beginning of 2001 came The Strokes: so perfectly New York new wave that had you photoshopped a picture of them onto a background of CBGB in 1979, you wouldn't have been able to fault their authenticity.

Lead track 'The Modern Age' was a perfect record for Geoff, who'd launched the Rough Trade shop in West London at the dawn of punk, importing records from the States, many of which probably shared the same urgent, breathless, short-form excitement that The Strokes specialised in.

Not just that, but like Elastica (and The Clash and other bands down the years we've namechecked), they looked like *a gang*. Effortlessly good-looking and not aloof, but unattainably cool. It was one of those instances when we didn't know what we were looking for until we found it.

By the spring of 2001, everyone, it seemed, was talking about The Strokes. Or at least they were in the UK. We couldn't play them enough. They recorded their first session and interview for us in February.

Interested in this new New York scene (and whether it existed at all), I went to stay in Manhattan for a few days, to hang around record shops and catch up with a couple of friends. Early one evening, I met one of them who worked in the music business in a bar on Avenue A, a small candlelit hang-out that she sometimes frequented.

"So what's going on in England then?" she asked.

"Well, The Strokes," I said, obviously.

"Who?"

"The Strokes," I repeated, a little flummoxed this time. "The Strokes... The Strokes, they come from here."

She gave me a blank look. The Strokes, it turned out, like the Fun Lovin' Criminals and others before them, weren't setting Manhattan alight as we might have imagined. In fact, while we were foaming at the mouth over their loose, buzzing power pop in the UK, New York was blissfully unaware that it had sold us a band whose album sleeve design would adorn thousands of teenage bedroom walls within months and who would inadvertently start a chain of musical events that would have an impact for the next two decades.

"Honestly, you're not winding me up. You've never heard of The Strokes."

"No."

And the conversation moved on, until about 15 minutes later, when I held my hand up (surely the international sign of 'Ssssshhhh') and said: "Hang on... this is them. This is The Strokes."

'Modern Age' was playing over the bar's stereo. Curious and now a bit confused, I went across and spoke to the sole bartender. "Sorry... but this is The Strokes, isn't it?"

"Yeah... how do you know? Where are you from?"

I explain. She looks taken aback. Another ten minutes later, a newly arrived guy, tall and with lightly tended bed-head hair, wanders over to our table and says: "You know The Strokes?"

I explain again. But this time it turns out I'm explaining how I know The Strokes to the manager of The Strokes, who co-owns the bar I'm sitting in.

A little later he returns and hands me his mobile. On the other end of the line is Albert Hammond Jr: "Hey... what the hell are you doing in our bar?"

It is simplifying the course of indie-rock history, I know, but the success of The Strokes was another turning point. It put Rough Trade back on top and it opened the way for another of their signings, The Libertines (superficially the British Strokes and another band who looked and walked like a gang, but who had a very English topspin with a manifesto and a back story – as if they'd been created by a drama writer with soap opera leanings).

Born out of a little scene, based around East London venue the Rhythm Factory, where they took up a sporadic and chaotic residency for a while, The Libertines arrived with their concept of The Albion (named after the archaic word for Great Britain): a fictional rock'n'roll ship that they would sail into the murky waters of pop, a symbol of Britishness that embodied comedian Tony Hancock, English literature of the fifties and sixties and vintage black-and-white films where men still wore bowler hats.

If The Strokes were what the New York Dolls had been to punk – a crackling spark of New York energy – then as a reaction, The Libertines were quite possibly our early noughties version of the Sex Pistols. They brought the rush of agitated guitar pop back to dear old Blighty, giving it some clearly signposted British references.

And if The Strokes were untouchable, then The Libertines were a little shambolic and vulnerable (used well, vulnerability and a general sense of haplessness can be a very attractive characteristic for some people). They were also reliably unpredictable. After the Leeds gig I saw them several times in and around London, and you never knew which Libertines were going to turn up – if they turned up at all! They became notorious for no shows or late stage times.

But whichever one it was, The Libertines – and maybe this is one of the things I gravitated to, on a personal level – inspired a loyalty among their fans that reminded me of the loyalty to bands I felt in my youth. One of my best friends, Tom Lissimore, was one of the Libs followers who would travel miles to a rumoured secret gig (or 'guerrilla gig', as they were dubbed), all the while wondering if they would show up but having decided it was worth the risk, *just to be there*.

But Tom's best Libertines tale is one of fandom *and* ingenuity. Tom arrived in Nottingham to go to university just as the venue the Rescue Rooms was opening. The Libertines were among the bands appearing in its first week, but tickets had long since sold out by the time Tom pitched up in his new home. Undeterred, he phoned up the venue the week before and said: "I see you're opening next week. Do you need any bar staff?"

"Actually, yes we do..."

On the night of The Libertines' gig, by accident, the venue had booked too many people for the bar, so they put Tom on the cloakroom – which, after everyone had arrived, he closed so he could go and watch the band.

The Libertines were probably the last big band we championed on *The Evening Session*. If you scout around online you can still find a couple of interviews from the show from 2002 which give a lovely reminder of what a tight-knit group they were – and how peculiarly English they sounded.

"We've lied about it so often it's difficult to remember how we did meet... but we can't lie to the BBC. That's illegal. It feels like everyone in Poplar has been in The Libertines at some point. We did lots of little residencies under lots of different names. It's been a pretty sordid affair really."

I loved the lyrical references to Tony Hancock, who was always on the radio when I was little, with repeats of his radio show; and I liked Pete Doherty's way of writing lyrics like he'd taken a bunch of Polaroids and cut them up and then reassembled them.

And their first album, *Up The Bracket*, had many of the qualities I hoped people had found in the debut Elastica album. In some ways, they were a good end point to the *Session*. It wasn't that we'd come round in a full circle, but we'd revisited the spirit of the early days of my and Jo's tenure on the show.

The Libertines would go on to be an influence on Arctic Monkeys, who, in turn, would become one of the major influences on the rest of the noughties – and far beyond.

By then, of course, *The Evening Session* – axed by the bosses at the end of 2002 for 'losing touch with the audience' – would be gone.

Although, in a twist of fate which I still can't quite believe, in that same year a new radio station launched that would harbour the whims and dreams and obsessions of music fans in a way I hadn't ever imagined.

And on October 16, my birthday, in 2002, I presented my first show for BBC Radio 6 Music. I followed a programme presented by former *NME* colleague Stuart Maconie. And I started it with Thin Lizzy's 'The Boys Are Back In Town'.

Outro

Of all my senses, the one that's survived and is still the most evocative is hearing. For some of my friends it's smell. They only have to catch a whiff of, say, mashed potato and they're transported back to primary school. My own sense of smell is appalling, and my taste isn't much better... but my hearing works.

Physically, I imagine it must be deteriorating (I've noticed I've had to turn my headphones up a touch over the last year to compensate). But otherwise it works amazingly well. I only have to play certain records and I'm whisked away in space and time. For instance: 'Love Cats' by The Cure. Early eighties. Benny's Disco, Harlow Student Night. Completely failed to get off with Elaine Westley.

'Strawberry Fields Forever' by Candy Flip: back of a car listening to a pirate radio station coming home from seeing the Senseless Things in Bath.

'Born Slippy' by Underworld: the *NME* tent at Reading Festival. I can hear the beat thumping through the canvas as my friend Neil Pengelly and I bowl up backstage on his scooter.

'The First Big Weekend' by Arab Strap: the old shoebox office Jo and I used to share at Radio 1's previous HQ in Egton House. My incredibly messy desk and the towering piles of cassettes.

'Mansize Rooster' by Supergrass: Sheffield town centre. Ben Wardle and I have been to see Supergrass supported by The

231

Bluetones in Manchester the previous night and have gone on to see Sleeper in Sheffield. We spend two hours roaming record shops looking for a red vinyl version of 'Mansize Rooster' before it starts pissing down and we have to shelter in a pub.

'I Get Along' by The Libertines: the final ever *Evening Session*.

'Helicopter' by Bloc Party: the Islington Academy. First on with The Coral. To my dismay, none of my friends liked them.

'Kiss With A Fist' by Florence & The Machine: SXSW 2008. During this song she ended up rolling around in the venue's water feature, before finishing the set by crawling underneath the stage.

'Well Done' by Idles: quite drunk in the Mothers Ruin pub in Bristol, where I met the band for the first time. Guitarist Bowen reveals his day job is being a dentist.

The list goes on and on.

Virtually every record I've ever bought has probably got some baggage attached to it. And despite the occasional downside (the records that remind me of times when things weren't going so well), I love the way they arouse all these emotions and images. I like the fact that in times of need I can go to my record collection and select a tune for all occasions (victorious, angry, sad, Saturday morning, Sunday evening, Colchester win, Colchester lose). The only problem with them is that I know what they do. I know how all these records will make me feel. There's no element of surprise.

That's why it's the music of tomorrow that will always have the upper hand. You just never know what's out there – or what it's going to sound like. And though I still need my comfort blanket albums, I have to own up and say, yes, I'd take the ultimate gamble. I really would swap one of the albums I know for one that hasn't even been released yet.

I'm not sure how I explain it, but you know when a friend says, "I remember hearing X record for the first time." And they tell you how taken aback by it they were; how they virtually fainted with excitement. Well, that's it. But it's not *remembering* the first time you heard a record, it's the actual first-time experience itself. That's the thing. That's why the pile of unlistened-to singles by the desk holds just as much fascination as the racks of dutifully filed albums behind it.

For fans like us, it's not just a question of "Do you remember the first time?" It's also the anticipation of the next time.

Acknowledgements

Many thanks to:

John and Peggy, Tom Lissimore, Chris North, Steve Backman at Primary Talent, Simon Williams, Neil Pengelly, Penny Blackham and Matt Silcox, Gillian Porter and the team at Hall Or Nothing, Jamie O'Hara, Chris 'The Pilot' Jackson, Kevin McCabe, Rob Lynch, Frank and everybody @theshipfitzrovia, Nigel and Joanne and the regulars at The Stags Head, James Chapple, Joe Mallott, Jan and Mac, Caroline and David, Monica Wolf, John Roddison and everyone who's looked after us at Brown McLeod, The Old Red Lion (Kennington), Steve Cooke, Greg Fountain, Keith Cameron, Laurence Bell, Mark Henwood.

Also: Jeff Smith, Mark Goodier and Matthew Bannister for giving me such support in the early days at the BBC. And to all the good folk at BBC6Music past and present.

All the photographers who have let us use their pictures.

Everyone who made this at Omnibus Press: David Barraclough, Imogen Gordon Clark, Raissa Pardini, Debra Geddes and Dave Stock.

This time, this one is for the girls: Jennifer Wills and Elizabeth Memphis Lamacq.

Steve Lamacq, Kennington 2019. Up The U's.